Time Management for Moms and Other Executives

JULIE AND CHARLES FONBUENA

DIVINATIVE LEADERSHIP

Acknowledgements

A big thanks to our children, Leslie, Nathan, Lauren, Leilani, Lindcee, Spencer and Benjamin who have had patience with us as we try to parent, and for being willing to let us "practice" on them.

Also, a special thanks to the mentors in our lives: first and foremost to our parents, Leonard & Yvonne Heaton and Leopoldo & Pilar Fonbuena, who have always believed in us; second, to our professional mentors, Chuck Farnsworth and John Covey who gave us vision and the courage to "be" more.

And most of all, we give our gratitude to God, for directing our lives in His way, in spite of our attempts to do it our own way.

Contents

TIME MANAGEMENT FOR MOMS AND OTHER EXECUTIVES

Pilot your life to a culture of being more and not just doing more.

Father might work from sunrise to sunset, but mother's work is never done.

—Author Unknown

THE reason why a mother's work is never done is because a mother's work has been inaccurately defined. Some may define a mother's work as a continual series of to-do lists with their starts and stops. For example, when a mother takes her child to a soccer game and the referee blows the final whistle, the game is done. When the groceries are brought in from the car and stored where they belong, the food shopping is done. When her child, asking for help with homework is taught, and the assignment is completed, her work as a tutor is done. Some would inaccurately define not just a mother's (and father's) work but also her worth, simply by the length of back-to-back activities strung together. By this warped definition, the work of a mother can never be done. Even though much of a mother's work is simply and remarkably a continual series of never-ending activities that flow from one thing to the next, that is not the point. Motherhood is more than just doing one project after another. The valuable work of a mother is not defined by the number of activities that can be strung together. From a child's point of view, a mother is not appreciated for the length of her to-do lists, but by the culture she builds for her family, and more especially, how one feels as a part of that culture. Just as an artist is not judged by the number of tubes of paint he uses, but by the quality and beauty of his paintings, a mother is not valued by the number of things she checks off her to-do list, but by the legacy she builds along the way and leaves behind.

To watch a mother's work is like watching the surf come in to shore. We don't appreciate the waves in the sea simply by counting how many waves have come in to shore or how fast. Instead we appreciate the entire experience. There are low tides, high tides, windswept or calm, different seasons, and varying sizes of waves. We remember the scents, the breeze, the sounds, the sand, the memories, the feelings, and the effect on the soul. Yet these waves always come to shore 24/7, night or day, rain or shine, from sunrise to sunset, and back again. Like watching and listening to the surf from a tropical beach in the summertime, a mother's continuous work is inspiring, wonderful, breathtaking, and amazing to behold. Have you ever just sat on the beach and looked at the waves for a while and said to yourself, "Wow!"? That's what a mother's work is like: you have to pause and pay close attention to fully appreciate it. You don't define a mother's work in terms of *doing*—but in terms of *being*.

Yet, we live in a busy world and getting things done is a big part of our lives. As in many areas of life, we use tools to help us be more efficient, and so it is with time management. So how do you create a time management tool and strategy for the kind of stewardship (motherhood) that is by its very nature—endless?

Many demands of life can complicate motherhood. Some have to juggle single motherhood, children with special needs, blended families, the workplace, and so forth. Though not nearly as endless a job as motherhood, the demands of the workplace are ever increasing in a competitive and global economy. With each passing year, many of our roles may tend to become more taxing, inching ever closer to the busyness and constancy that is found in the role of motherhood. The pressures of our occupations or businesses consume our time, thoughts, and activities long after the office has closed. It would be great to find out how the most effective moms handle wave after wave of never-ending demands of motherhood, because similar demands are headed towards all of us. Regardless of the nature of our lives, we all need to deal with and redefine the same finite and important resource—time. How do we best use our time to lead fulfilling lives?

CHAPTER ONE

WHY MOST TIME-MANAGEMENT TOOLS DON'T WORK

WHEN introduced to my first time-management tool, I was resistant, because I thought time planners are for nerds. I was perfectly content to go about my life without one. All of a sudden I found myself working for a company that was teaching time management to clients. I decided that I had better use one, so I would know what I was talking about. Surprisingly, the more I used my time-management tool, the more I got done, because I was more organized. I wasn't forgetting events, details on assignments, nor important dates and appointments. The increased productivity was great, but it got to the point where I felt that instead of using my planner, my planner was using me. I got more and more done, but was experiencing *less* fulfillment and balance. I tried to convince myself that my life was *more* fulfilled and balanced, but my family saw things differently. The more I got done, the more I realized how much I wasn't getting done and how much I needed to get done the next day. The work load was ever-increasing, and the information was coming at me from all angles at an accelerating rate. The more I put into my work life, the less I put into my family life, both in time as well as focus. This merry-go-round I was on kept going faster and faster. My days were more dizzying, and I wasn't sure how to get off that crazy ride. Can you relate?

Too many people begin using a planner simply because everyone else is doing it. Once they start living life according to their planners, many people find that nothing creates imbalance in their lives faster than a time-management tool that was intended to keep track of all their activities, appointments, and so forth. The efficiency was supposed to free up more time, which would then give us more opportunity for life balance. For most, it hasn't worked out way. Why?

Skewed Towards One Role

People usually find that their planners are skewed towards one role—most often it is the work role. How do I use my time so that I can survive and ultimately thrive to meet my physical and financial needs? Our time management tool can be just a survival tool—how to survive at work and how to survive at home. Some planners have components to balance the different roles in their lives, but it seldom happens. The more time and effort that is spent to organize and complete career goals, the more their other priorities become neglected, from taking care of oneself, caring for one's family, to nurturing other important relationships and roles. There is another usually unintended consequence of having a disproportionate amount of attention, time and planning devoted towards one role. Though we may profess that our work is not our life, when we put that much emphasis on one role, it becomes that much easier to make work the center of our lives, even if that is not our intention. Somewhere along the way, the other roles (even family roles) can become mere distractions.

In a conversation with work colleagues, one of them commented that there is nothing easier than being a workaholic. You have one area of focus, where you can excel and are rewarded for excellence. There is not the need to mentally and emotionally shift your attention to other roles and responsibilities on a daily basis. It is also easy to rationalize the need to just keep on working, citing "responsibilities at work" and "we need the money" or "the sacrifice now will help us get what we ultimately want later." Yes, our time-management tool has the ability to help us focus on work. Unfortunately, that kind of time-management tool can *indefinitely* keep us focused on work as well. Being a workaholic is a simpler life, but not a completely fulfilling or balanced one.

Focused Almost Exclusively on Tasks and Appointments

Another reason time-management tools can create imbalance for many people is because they are often focused almost exclusively on tasks and appointments. It is as if we have become human "doings" as opposed to human "beings." More often than not, we pose the question of what to "do," but seldom ask, what in the end, will we "be" as a result of all the doing. Accomplishing things and checking them off our lists is a part of who we are, but it is not all that we are. Admittedly, we sometimes define ourselves in terms of what we have achieved. Think of your response when someone asks you, "What do you do?" Do you think and answer in terms of primarily your profession, your title, or the organization you are associated with? Humor me for a moment and point to yourself.

Look at where you are pointing. Are you pointing to your brain, your wallet, your stomach, or your feet? Chances are you weren't pointing at any of these, but more than likely, you pointed to your heart instead. Interesting isn't it? We may describe who we are by what we do professionally, but we identify who we are by pointing to the heart!

Let's go back to accomplishing tasks. We love doing and accomplishing, because when we accomplish a task there are endorphins—chemicals are sent to our brains that make us feel good for having completed something. We get an added emotional boost the more we can put check marks on a piece of paper next to our accomplished tasks. The unexamined paradigm is, if I accomplish something that makes me feel good, doesn't it make sense that accomplishing more would make me feel that much better? Not necessarily. If you are not careful, you can find yourself in the proverbial scenario of straightening out the deck chairs in the Titanic as it is going down. You can find yourself busy, but not heading in the direction of where you eventually want to be. Have you ever examined your to-do-lists at the end of the day, and even though there is a sense of satisfaction from finishing a number of tasks, sometimes deep down you feel as if you have not done anything of significance?

I was talking with a very successful executive. His position required a great deal of international travel. The promotions and all of the perks and benefits that went with those promotions were coming fast. However, his job was taking quite a toll on his family, and he felt that he was becoming more distant with each member of his family. To complicate matters, all the travel was also taking a toll on his physical well-being. The constant travel overseas was adversely affecting his back and shoulders. He confided in me that the job was exciting, but when he thought of the price he had paid in his relationships and his body, he felt it was no longer worth it. I asked him if he had thought of an exit strategy from his dilemma, and with a puzzled look he said, "I hadn't even considered that."

Accomplishing tasks and having the satisfaction of doing more can feel great, but there is a point where doing more is just *more* and not necessarily *better*. It's been said that even virtue taken to an extreme can become a vice. Continually extending our to-do list would qualify for this. There is always a trade-off. With my executive friend, there was a point at which accomplishing more at work meant he had to pay a toll in his relationship with his family and a physical toll on his body. He needed a way out.

Here is something else to consider in our series of to-do lists. For many people, the relationships that are built and strengthened in the workplace are done simply as the "means" to the end. In other words we build relationships so that other people can help us get things done. The goal is to accomplish "tasks, projects, or goals." At first glance there may be nothing wrong with this idea. It's simply a matter of delegating people to different roles and responsibilities. This way of operating becomes a problem, however, when we get so used to it that we have the same mindset in all our roles. We build relationships for the sole purpose of accomplishing tasks. This is sometimes referred to as "using people." This may sound harsh, but not as harsh as the potential consequences of actually using people.

During a very important conversation with my son, exasperated, he said, "Dad, don't talk to me like I'm one of your employees. I'm your son." If we are not careful, when circumstances call for having tasks and activities to build relationships, we may have it backwards, and only build relationships to accomplish tasks and goals. People can become merely the means to an end. Consider that we sometimes refer to people as human resources. Think about that phrase "human resources" for a minute. People can become resources much like equipment, buildings, tools, and desks. Much like equipment, buildings, and other capital expenditures, the value of individuals can be viewed as depreciating in value over time. People can even be thought of as eventually becoming obsolete. It's also interesting that in a company's financial statement items such as inventory, buildings, and equipment are referred to as assets, and people are in the section called expenses. We are more than human doings and human resources. We are human beings.

If I'm Organized Enough, I Can Accomplish All Things—Not!

Somewhere along the line we have entertained the notion that if we are organized enough, then we can accomplish all things. If we are organized enough and really manage our time well, we can go to bed at night knowing that all things that can be accomplished, have been accomplished, and the following day brings a whole new beginning. I can convince myself into thinking that if I'm organized enough I can begin each day with a blank slate with nothing left over from yesterday. We expect almost a mechanical life where there are starts and stops, on and off. This is one of the unexamined mindsets that if not addressed, can increase our frustration the more we use our time management tool. It can leave you feeling like the dog chasing its own tail. We might be moving quickly but not moving forward. It is unrealistic to expect that organization alone will lead to an effective life. I know we don't actually believe this. We just hope in the back of our minds that it might be that simple. Being organized is helpful but not a panacea. We may wish life were more structured and predictable, but in reality our lives are much more fluid now than ever.

Not Designed for Life Balance

Time management tools are usually not designed to define nor produce balance. In fact balance is usually left out of the equation. How do you define life balance? When someone says the word *balance*, what visual representation comes to mind? For most people it's a scale. Therefore, most of us conclude that life balance must be a series of scales where we measure time spent in each role, and then quality of life is evaluated accordingly. If I put equal amounts of time into different roles, I conclude that I must be balanced. The weight and impact of the activities themselves is usually not considered. Simply making sure that time is spent in each role is what is valued. This is inaccurate and incomplete.

Look at balance instead in terms of dancing. The dancers achieve "balance" as they go through their routines, and they constantly shift their weight according to the dance moves, whether the style of dance is ballet, ballroom dancing, or street dancing. When it comes to time management, life balance is a series of rhythms and movements that accompany the melody of life. Some parts of the dance of life are fast and others slower. Some parts are taxing others relaxing. The dance of life as a whole, however, should bring us joy. As you revisit the definition of life balance in the context of a dance, you may be pleasantly surprised that life is going better than you thought. If not, I hope a change in definition will help you redefine the problem as well as the solution.

In each person's life there are periods of temporary imbalance that eventually lead to overall life balance. For example, how many of you have ever felt you were out of balance as a college student or when you were getting specialized training for your profession? Yet that temporary imbalance of college life or training allows you to have opportunities now, that you may not have had otherwise. How many of you with children, have ever felt temporary imbalance when your first child was born? Sleep deprived? Did your life revolve around your infant child? Did you stay up after the toddler finally went to sleep, just to take a moment in silence to stare at your child in awe and wonder? The precious but exhausting time spent with your infant child, literally changes your outlook on life. Your infant child probably redefined what the word *balance* means for you. In a different stage of life, how many of you have stayed up late at night into the early morning having meaningful discussions with your teenagers? You may remember feeling the exhausting physical effects of those late nights, but they may also be the moments when those relationships are built and strengthened. In these moments creating a schedule and sticking to it is laughable. We all just learn to go with the flow, and that's okay.

How many of you have had longs days at work when you were given a new assignment or were promoted? You were anxious to do a good job, and you made sure you got through the critical learning curve as quickly as possible. Your efforts have paid dividends. The key is to make sure these temporary imbalances, are indeed *temporary*. When the temporary imbalances of your life never cease, you'll get burned out. How long can you dance at a fast pace before you get sick of dancing and sick of the music as well? Life balance is a dance. There are varying speeds, movements, and intensity. Live your life in such a way that you enjoy the music along the way.

Relationships and Values Not Part of the Tool

Most people don't incorporate their relationships and their values or character traits into their time management planning process—even though if asked, they would say they want to prioritize those relationships and live by those values and character traits. Slowly and almost imperceptibly, you can lose focus on your values without even recognizing it until a lot of time has been lost. As we will examine in greater detail, the development of our character affects what we do, say, and ultimately achieve.

> The bitterest tears shed over graves are for words left unsaid and deeds left undone.
>
> —Harriet Beecher Stowe

Robert Frost had a similar caution from his poem "The Road Not Taken." Most people remember the last lines:

> Two roads diverged in a wood, and I—
> I took the one less traveled by,
> And that has made all the difference.

There's another part of the poem that is worth another look and can also make all the difference. Remember the line,

> Yet knowing how way leads on to way, I doubted if I should ever come back.

For those of us who have experienced what "way leads on to way" means, there is hope and a plan. To me, "way leads on to way" means, you take an unexpected turn in your life's journey, and it becomes your life. Maybe your career finds you in a place you never imagined, and you don't feel you belong there. Perhaps your family life is not what you had envisioned while growing up or considered even in the courtship years. You may not be able to go back in time, but you can certainly lead your life and your time to be the person you've always wanted to be, even if there are detours. We'll take a deliberate approach in making sure, your most important relationships and your deeply-held values are part of your time management philosophy. The intent is to add to the strengths of common time-management strategies such as putting down lists of tasks organized in days, times, and priorities, and integrate them with strategies that will help each of us become the person we want to be.

The most dominant governing value that is built into the current time management tools, without us perhaps even realizing it, is speed and efficiency. When someone touts the promise of speed and efficiency it gets our attention. However, weightier matters such as values and mission may be omitted. In rare cases, values and mission may be part of the instruction manual or even the seminar on time management, but more often than not, values and mission are not a part of the time management system itself. Again, speed and efficiency are nice, only after values and purpose are in place. That's our goal.

Taking these five reasons altogether, it is not difficult to see why many people don't persist in using their planners or become dissatisfied in using them. Some very important components are missing. If there are fundamental flaws in the time-management approach and its results, then it's difficult to develop it into a habit. We still want to find something that really works, but in the meantime, we just resolve to do the best we can with what we have.

> The significant problems we face cannot be solved at the same level of thinking we were at, when we created them.
>
> —Albert Einstein

The first order of business is to examine the nature of these time-management problems and how it is, as Albert Einstein put it, that we have created them. Unlike most time management books, articles, and seminars, the focus of this book is not on the mechanical aspects of time management, but rather on examining our individual beliefs and character, and then integrating character into the way we manage our time and activities. This is about making sure we are headed in the right direction and tapping into the very best within each of us. This is in contrast to focusing on speed and assuming the direction is accurate and will miraculously manifest itself later.

If you are one who:

- Uses your time-management tool religiously
- Feels guilty about not using your time-management tool more consistently
- Has thought many times about getting a time-management tool but haven't got around to it
- Gags at even the thought of using a time-management tool

Take a deep breath. Be open to examining a new way of thinking about time management. Solving significant problems takes more than just doing the opposite of what was done before. Rather, it first takes a whole new approach toward defining the problem and an innovative way to solving it. When it comes to your time-management tool, in the end you will use a system that works best for your situation and helps you to be become the person you want to be.

CHAPTER TWO

GENESIS OF THIS BOOK

THE genesis of this book came from having a very insightful wife, combined with my work as an independent consultant. I've worked with private as well as public companies. I've conducted workshops with schools, churches, and government entities. I've worked with small businesses to multi-national corporations. Coming home from my consulting work, from time to time I would ask my wife her opinions and insights on the leadership and time-management content I facilitate. Participants often ask how leadership and time management principles that apply in the workplace, would apply in the home. Wanting to make sure I gave very pragmatic answers to my clients rather than just theories, I would solicit my wife's wisdom and feedback.

Such a conversation produced one of her choice observations: "You share wonderful things with your clients, and I can see how it applies to them. But some things don't seem quite on the mark from my vantage point." Surprised, I pressed her a bit more. Then she gave this pithy remark:

If it doesn't apply in the home keep working on it.

I thought: *Wow! Now there's a brilliant idea.* She then shared how she could imagine that clients can see how leadership and time-management concepts can be on the mark when it comes to applying them in the workplace, but slightly off the mark when it comes to applying them at home. To illustrate, I remember seeing a humorous cartoon of a father, mother, and four little children sitting around the dining table. The father, still in his business attire, called a family meeting. The caption then said in effect, "I have called this family meeting to announce that because of the recent economic downturn, I'm afraid I'm going to have to let a couple of you go!"

Meetings to announce downsizing may apply in the work environment but not so much in the home. This is just one facetious example of what my wife was alluding to when she mentioned business practices not necessarily being applicable in the home. As I speak to private and public organizations, I see some of them sitting there approvingly listening to my presentation regarding their work concerns. Yet, I suspect that all the while their minds and hearts drift to concerns at home. They wonder how improvements at work could translate to improvements at home. Participants try to reconcile the all-too-common gap between challenges at work and challenges at home.

I've often reflected on my wife's comment and have appreciated its great merit. The content I was teaching was very good, but it didn't go far enough. My wife's comment kept coming back: *If it doesn't apply in the home, keep working on it.* Home is so vitally important to each of us. After all, the home is where we experienced our first job through chores, first school with a parent's tutoring, our first hospital as a parent nursed our first wounds, first social interactions with parents and siblings, first sports event through playing, first church through a parent's sermon, and first party for whatever it was we were celebrating. The home is where we first get a sense of our self-worth, belonging, and identity. The home is where we develop our sense and mental blueprints of how things should be. In the end, the home is where our most valued relationships are, long after our careers are over. From the beginning to the end of our lives, we long for home. So leadership and time management concepts only have great value if they apply as effectively in the home as at work. If our time-management strategy can simultaneously improve both home life and work life, then we feel that our whole lives are really moving forward, as opposed to feeling that our work lives and home lives are being ripped apart and moving in opposite directions. People are likely to remember those concepts and apply them consistently into the future, because they will find that doing so improves all aspects of their lives.

On the other hand, if our time management methodology isn't equally as effective at home as at work, we will more readily dismiss it. Even though we have many roles to juggle, we're not interested in a separate time-management strategy for each role. If we don't dismiss our flawed time-management methodology, we are at the least, lukewarm towards it. We halfheartedly try something, rationalizing that life can be so chaotic and stressful that trying *something* has to be better than *nothing*. All the while we keep on searching. We want something that integrates all parts of our lives. We search for simplicity in life while removing complexity in our time-management tools. We also want something that truly helps us—something that we intuitively know makes sense. We're not interested in bells and whistles, as much as truly developing ourselves and progressing to become the people we want to be, while helping those we care deeply about do the same.

This book evolved from the synergies of insights from nature, observations from daily living and the workplace, as well as thoughts from mothers in varying stages of life on dealing with a challenge that we all face constantly—time management. It is called *Time Management for Moms and Other Executives,* because as a society, we hold executives in high regard given their status, scope of responsibilities, and the impact they can make. We're curious to know how they view the world differently and what lessons we might glean from their experience. We'll share some of those executive insights.

When I think of status, responsibility, and impact, however, no one comes close to a mother. Conduct your own personal survey and ask your family members, friends, and colleagues this one simple question:

From your earliest recollection until today, who have been the most influential people in your life?

Create your list and have your family members, friends, and colleagues do the same. Compare the lists and see who shows up most often. Who would you anticipate would most often make the list of the most influential person in most people's lives? An executive? Work associate? A neighbor? Teacher? Friend? Family members? Or Mother? Mother (and father) shows up in an overwhelming majority of the time. It is amazing the impact our mothers have on each of us, even long after we have moved away from home. We still feel the influence of our mothers long after they have passed away. Interestingly, Mother's Day is observed in most countries around the world. The impact of mothers is known and felt worldwide regardless of race, language, religion, or political affiliation. The impact executives have by the decisions they make, may be significant and immediate, and it may even last for decades, but the impact of mothers and fathers is measured in generations. Just the very thought of motherhood commands respect, reverence, and honor. Because motherhood has such a universal impact, there are great lessons to be learned as to what they do with such unconscious competence. Moms are executives indeed, and the most effective executives run their companies like a family. Whether at home or at work, every family member and work associate wants to feel valued. All want to feel that they are growing, that they belong, and that they are making a significant contribution. Mothers have to run an organization—the family—with personalities and relationships as complex as those found in any corporation. The most effective executives have to learn to manage change, dichotomies, and paradoxes in their corporations and organizations that are as complex as those found in a home. We'll tap into insights from moms and executives and address the following questions as well as others.

- How do I balance time for work, time for family and extended family, as well as time for myself?
- How can I possibly get everything done in an increasingly fast-paced world where demands are ever multiplying? I'm just talking about work. When I get home there's another set of demands I have to tackle. There's still cooking, cleaning, homework with my kids, and each family member's challenge for the day. I feel both overwhelmed by what needs to be done and guilty for not accomplishing everything.
- When will I ever have time to create a culture of responsibility, caring, improvement, along with all of the other qualities that I want for my home as well as other roles?
- I have so much to do, yet my challenges are small compared to friends and loved ones, and I feel bad for not getting around to helping them. What can I do?
- Why can't I get as much done as I see others doing?
- How do I keep from getting burned out and discouraged? I feel that I am shouldering heavy burdens all alone.
- I use a planning tool and have increased my productivity, but I don't feel like I'm getting closer to the person I want to be. It seems at times that I'm getting more done at one end, yet I see my life unraveling on the other end.

Sound familiar?

As you go through this book, you will not only discover that these problems are solvable, but you will rediscover that there is much to celebrate about what you are already doing. As you read, you will recognize that not only are these concepts easy to understand, but you may have already applied them in your life—even if it was not done deliberately or consistently. Many people do apply these concepts with unconscious competence. A fresh perspective, however, and a very deliberate and holistic approach will make all the difference.

THE ESSENCE OF THIS BOOK

I wouldn't give a fig for the simplicity this side of complexity,
but I'd give my life for the simplicity on the far side of complexity.
—Justice Oliver Wendell Holmes

Let me give the simplicity of this book after the complexity is all said and done. It is simply this:

Adjust your time management practice with the intent to *pilot* your life to a *culture* of focusing on *being* more and not just *doing* more. Create this culture for yourself, for your family, and for every other role you may have.

BEING

I like the word *being* as opposed to *becoming*. Much as an apple seed isn't going to become or somehow be transformed into a rose bush, likewise we are not trying to become nor do we intend to be altered into something else. Existing within each person are intelligence, capacity, and the potential to be great—all anxious to manifest. We are each intended to fully realize our already-divine nature instead of trying to figure out what else we may become. Our potential as human beings is magnificent, and our contributions can be significant when we fully tap into that potential. Focus on *being* first, and the appropriate *doing* will come. Keep in mind that the doing is only one component of potential. We'll explore this in more detail later. With most time management practices, it is so easy to get lost in *doing* more, that we lose track of why we do what we do in the first place.

We are more than to-do lists and goal setting. We each have a compassionate heart, a divine mind, an eternal spirit, beloved relationships, as well as a body that can accomplish tasks. We each have a personal life, family life, work life, and other roles in our communities. We have dreams, aspirations, fears, and doubts. This book is about reconciling all of these in the midst of an ever-changing world with its accelerating pace. On occasion we may even have our lives reconciled and be at peace with everything, but our time management tools are going in different directions. The idea is to get alignment on all these facets of our lives and *be* the people we want to be.

Bishop Vaughn J. Featherstone recalls hearing a story of the son of King Louis XVI of France. It is wonderful illustration of what it means to be the person we want to be.

King Louis had been taken from his throne and imprisoned. His young son, the prince, was taken by those who had dethroned the king. They thought that inasmuch as the king's son was heir to the throne, if they could destroy him morally, he would never realize the great and grand destiny that life had bestowed upon him.

They took him to a community far away, and there they exposed the lad to every filthy and vile thing that life could offer. They exposed him to foods the richness of which would quickly make him a slave to appetite. They used vile language around him constantly. They exposed him to lewd and lusting women. They exposed him to dishonor and distrust. He was surrounded twenty-four hours a day by everything that could drag the soul of a man as low as one could slip. For over six months he had this treatment—but not once did the young lad buckle under pressure. Finally, after intensive temptation, they questioned him. Why had he not submitted himself to these things—why had he not partaken? These things would provide pleasure, satisfy his lusts, and were desirable; they were all his. The boy said, "I cannot do what you ask for I was born to be a king."

Every person has nobility within himself or herself. Every person is a king or a queen in his or her own right. Every person was born to be a ruler and leader of his or her own life, destined to make a significant contribution. We all aspire to be the very best we can be. How would we all lead our lives and use our time differently if we truly knew that we were destined to be great? How would we perceive and treat our family members or others, if we saw the greatness in them as well? How would we use our time differently to help our family and others rise to the nobility that is in them? I realize we live in a world where there are those whose current lives are less than noteworthy, but don't we all wish to be seen in a better light, and don't we all long to be more? How do we pilot or navigate our lives towards this culture of being more and realize the nobility that is in each of us? We'll go through the thought process, skills, and tools to build a culture of being more and not just doing more.

CULTURE

If our intent is to build a culture of being more, what is the definition of culture? When I mention the word culture I am defining it as shared values. In other words, what do we *really* all share in common? Culture is what we collectively and similarly think and feel about each other when we are together. What kind of culture do you want to build and be part of? Let's take a look at culture as it applies at work as well as the home.

Work Culture

Consider this hypothetical work scenario. In the work environment, for instance, a team is assembled in which each member has great ideas, and they each vary in their personalities, roles, experience, and abilities. Everyone seems friendly and cordial, but when asked to share their best practices and ideas, they rarely share their very best ideas, because they know they may not get the credit for their ideas. Others don't share their ideas because they don't trust each other. Others only share ideas when they are fully developed instead of trusting a process of developing ideas together. Because the boss is the one asking for ideas, everyone speaks up, but they don't share their very best ideas—just their mediocre ones. As a consequence, most ideas are a rehash of the last meeting, because they want to retain a personal competitive advantage within the team and get the individual bonus or recognition. One particular team member may have a great idea, but he'll save it for a private meeting with the boss and receive full recognition and attention from the boss. What is the shared value in this instance? *Working independently* and *competition*! The team leader may even talk about the benefits of teamwork, and there may even be a plaque on the wall talking about the declared values of *teamwork, cooperation,* and *collaboration,* but the value that is really shared by all or the more accurate culture that exists is *internal competition.*

The executive's first job is to create a culture where its stated values are truly what the behaviors and attitudes say it is, and not just what the plaques and business cards say it is. If the culture or value that is shared by all is positive, then everything else can be built on that foundation. If not, then cynicism develops and spreads like a metastasizing cancer. To the executives or for any manager having stewardships over other people, here is the question: *Are we focused on building the culture we want, or is our time-management context limited to a to-do list for the day?*

Family Culture

Building and cultivating a healthy culture or shared value is equally important in the home. The primary job of parents is to decide and then to build what they would like as the family culture or shared values. To illustrate, my wife comes from a large family and extended family. Let me clarify what I mean by large. When my wife's grandfather passed away over fifteen years ago he was survived by ten children, sixty-five grandchildren, and over one hundred great grand-children. Of course, the family is much larger than that now.

Every summer there is a weekend family reunion, and families come from all over the United States. When you have an extended family of this size and add to it the in-laws, you will have all the diversity of opinions, socio-economic demographics, education, and experience imaginable. The family reunions are always held in a beautiful lush ranch in the backdrop of Bryce National Park. The ranch has been in the family for many years. There are two cabins on the ranch, and in front of one of the cabins is a large wooden porch at the edge of a pond. The water in the pond is supplied from a mountain stream. Because there are only two cabins and a large family, you come prepared with your camping gear for the weekend in the event you aren't lucky enough or early enough to get a room in the cabins. Before going to my first family reunion, my wife tried to prepare me as much as possible, as to what I should expect. Of course the biggest adjustment was seeing the sheer size of the gathering. The running joke between my wife and me as we would meet everyone at the ranch was, "Oh honey, you remember so and so. They were at our wedding." Right!

On Friday night, after the initial shock of seeing so many people at a family reunion, we were getting ready to go to sleep on our little tent. I asked my wife what I should expect on Saturday. She said the setting is very casual and nothing is scheduled other than the meals. Certain families are assigned to prepare the meals for everyone, and the assignments rotate yearly. She said everyone gets up pretty early. The children play games and the adults talk and mingle. Then she gave me the proverbial, "Oh yeah and one more thing" speech. She said when people come to the ranch for the first time, at some point during Saturday the uncles and cousins will gather around you, hold and swing you by your wrists and ankles, and from the porch they'll throw you into the pond! You can run if you like, she said, and that's part of the fun, but know that with hundreds of people chasing you down, it's impossible to get away. I asked her if anyone was exempt from being thrown in. She said there are only a few exceptions. You have to be a great grandparent, sick, injured, or pregnant.

Not wanting to get thrown in the pond, the next morning I managed to commandeer and put on a dress. With a pillow under the dress, I pretended to be pregnant. I made a sign that I hung around my neck. It read: *Ineligible for the pond*. Much of this large extended family was already awake and gathered together for an outdoor breakfast feast when I came on the scene complete with my outfit, my sign, and my best "I'm nine months pregnant" walk. There was laughter all throughout breakfast, and I could see the uncles and cousins in my peripheral view giving the signals to each other saying, "We'll throw him in the pond first." Shortly after breakfast I could sense that the hunt was on, and I made a run for it. I didn't get far, and into the pond I went. Did I mention that the water from the pond is supplied by a mountain stream? It was cold! I came out of the water to applause, and I was officially initiated into the family.

Throughout the day I made my rounds talking to the uncles, aunts, cousins, and in-laws, as well as the grandparents. I was observing the interactions within this large and diverse family, and concluded that the culture or shared value was acceptance. I felt accepted in my first experience at the family reunion and every time I have gone. I feel the same acceptance when I visit with extended family members in different settings. My children feel the same acceptance. My parents and siblings feel the acceptance as they mingle with my wife's extended family.

Think of different families that you may visit. Recall the feeling when you visit the homes of your extended family, friends, work colleagues, and neighbors. What would you say is the culture or the values they truly share in their homes? What do you think others would say is the shared value in your home? What would you like your family culture or shared values to be?

PILOT

Time and time again as I get on commercial flights, I always marvel at how a plane gets off the ground. It takes a great deal of effort, power, and know-how to achieve flight. Similarly, I am amazed as I watch so many people live their lives with great courage, consistency, and diligence. For all your efforts, however, have you ever felt at one time or another, as if your life seems to be in a holding pattern where you exert a great deal of effort, but in your heart of hearts you feel that your life is going in circles? Have you ever wondered why it is that even though you are still exerting a great deal of effort, power, and know-how—and may even be increasing speed—that your life isn't moving any further along than before? How do we not only navigate but pilot our lives to get out of the holding pattern and continually move towards our mission or the person we want to be? How do we analyze what caused us to get into the holding pattern in the first place and make sure it doesn't happen again?

The purpose of this book is to step back a bit and focus on piloting our lives to a culture that enables us individually and as families, to focus and use our time on *being* the people we want to be. This same strategy will also be helpful in all of the other important relationships and roles that we have, whether it's for work, volunteer roles, civic duties, or any other role.

CHAPTER THREE

REDEFINING THE TIME MANAGEMENT CHALLENGE

I started this book with the sentence, "The reason why a mother's work is never done is because a mother's work has been inaccurately defined." So what is the more accurate description of our time-management challenge? As I was trying to organize the insights I have learned from my consulting work and the insights I have learned from my wife and many other moms, I wanted to organize the concepts in this book as linearly as possible, hoping to make the understanding and applying of this time-management philosophy as easy as possible. I struggled with it for a while, because the nature of our time-management dilemma is not linear.

The easiest way to understand our time-management challenge is to look at it from a weaving metaphor. When weaving in a loom, there is a row of yarn that is placed vertically in the loom. These rows of yarn are collectively called the warp. The collective width of these vertical rows of yarn determines the width of the fabric. Each yarn that will make up the warp has to be strong enough to withstand being stretched and placed under tension. It's important to note that it takes effort just to get the warp set up, before the designs can be woven in. The yarn that crisscrosses at right angles or perpendicular to the warp yarn to create the design of the fabric is called the weft. The warp and the weft are equally important for the strength and integrity of the fabric. The warp and weft complement each other. Without one or the other, the fabric will unravel, and you will be left with just a lump of yarn. If the warp and weft are properly woven, they can form a strong and beautiful fabric.

As we apply this metaphor to time management, the weft represents all the activities we want to accomplish. Much as the weft can come in different designs and colors, we can choose to participate in any activity we want and design our lives however we want. In weaving, the width of the warp determines the width of the fabric, but the weft determines its length. You can make the weft as long as you want. The length is shorter when you are making scarves and obviously longer if you are making blankets. Similarly, the activities and goals we decide to take on can be as long or as short as we want. Longer doesn't necessarily mean better. It just depends on what it is you are trying to build.

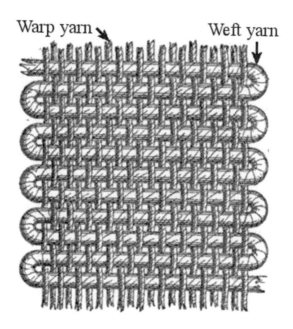

In our weaving metaphor, the warp represents our character. Much as the warp gives the fabric its strength, so our character gives our lives strength. Just as fabric can wear out quicker and unravel if the warp is not strong enough, so can our lives unravel if we don't give our character enough of our time to set up properly, to focus sufficiently and develop fully.

Character is that which reveals moral purpose, exposing the class of things a man chooses and avoids.

—Aristotle

Consider the lives of the so-called famous and successful people whose fame, fortune, and success are replaced with scandal, lost fortunes, damaged reputations, and broken families, because their integrity of character has been compromised. Such a tale is of course not limited to those who make headlines, but we are all subject to the same forces. Our lives can also unravel if we don't give sufficient focus on developing our character as well as achieving goals and completing our to-do lists. We are redefining our time-management challenge as, "How do we balance our time between developing character and using unique talents in ways that would make masterpieces of our lives?" This book is about using our time to weave together the warp of character and the weft of activities and goals. Just as a woven tapestry can beautify a room by its presence, so can we live lives of inspiration for others and fulfillment for ourselves when we build a culture of being more and not just doing more.

ROADMAP

So far we have covered the purpose and backdrop for a different approach to time management. We've examined why it is that much, if not all, of the current time-management philosophies don't work. We know the essence of this time-management book is to pilot our lives to a culture of being more and not just doing more. We have envisioned the weaving metaphor to help us redefine our time-management challenge and give us a picture of what we are trying to achieve. The next part of this book is laying out a couple of realities of life for you to consider deeply in chapter four. It will help you make the shift from thinking in terms of to-do lists to thinking in terms of to-be lists and being more. We'll examine how your brain works and how this affects the way you view your life, your priorities, and the motivations for your actions. In chapter five we will examine a second set of realities specifically regarding time management. These will be foundational to making further mental shifts from doing more to being more.

The remaining chapters will incorporate a series of allegories to illustrate and clarify. These allegories are also intended to make the concepts easier to remember. As we move from the first allegory to the last, we will be moving from the broadest philosophical strokes of time management in the first allegory, to suggesting very specific practices in the last allegory. Through these allegories, as our weaving metaphor suggests, we will explore just how interwoven time management is to character development and goal achievement. Through these allegories we will answer the following questions:

- Why is a focus on character development a necessary part of time management, and what difference does it make?
- Who are the people who can help us be the people we want to be, how essential are they, and how will we identify them?
- What are the vital roles that we need to balance, and how do we prioritize them?
- How will we achieve change, improvement, and results, and how do we align our time to consistently develop our character and achieve our goals?
- Where and how do I start in my quest to develop my character?
- When should I expect to see results?
- How do I implement all of this in a simple and powerful way?

At the end of each allegory you will compile your to-be list and consider a few activities to implement. You will have the opportunity to commit to your to-be action plan that will weave for your life the warp of character and weft of activities and goals. These to-be action plans will be part of your time management philosophy. These action plans are either specific things you can do at specific times or they can be areas of focus that are not time sensitive. In the sixth allegory you will use a time management tool that will incorporate all of these ideas in your life.

Let's get started!

CHAPTER FOUR

A COUPLE OF REALITIES OF LIFE

LET'S examine a couple of bedrock realities to build the foundation of being more and not just doing more. I call these two realities:

- Three Brains
- The Ugly Duckling

THREE BRAINS

The neurologist Paul MacLean has proposed in his book *The Triune Brain in Evolution,* that our skulls hold not one but three brains. You can look at them as three interconnected computers, where each computer has its own intelligence and memory.

MacLean refers to one part of the brain as the reptilian brain. It's also called the lower brain, and for the remainder of the book I'll refer to it as the lizard brain. This is the brain stem and cerebellum that controls the movement of our muscles as well as balance, breathing, and heartbeat. He refers to it as the reptilian brain, because with reptiles, this is the dominant portion of the brain; it controls their survival instincts, behavior, and thinking. It basically responds to two questions: *Can I eat it?* or *Can it eat me?* After those two questions are answered, the brain then operates on survival instincts and asks: *How do I conquer or escape from being conquered?*

The second brain he refers to the limbic system. It's also called the middle brain. The limbic system includes the amygdala, the hypothalamus, and the hippocampus. The limbic system has also been referred to as the mammalian brain, and for the remainder of the book I'll refer to it as the monkey brain. This part of the human brain is home to our emotions and moods. At the touch of an electrode, feelings of fear, pleasure, joy, and rage could be produced. In this limbic system or emotional system everything is either "agreeable or disagreeable." This is the part of the brain that tells us to avoid pain and repeat pleasure. This processing of emotions in the limbic system is also connected to how we interact with others. Just as there are social norms with monkeys, dolphins, and other mammals, this is the part of the brain that dictates the existence of certain rules when interacting with other people. This part of the brain reinforces the idea that if we want to satisfy our need and desire to belong and fit in with others, we need to follow the rule of the pack. When we feel that we belong in the pack, we feel better; when we feel that we are on the outside looking in and not part of the pack, we don't feel so good.

The third part of the human brain MacLean refers to as the neocortex. The neocortex makes up about two-thirds of the total brain mass of a human. In animals, however, it is much smaller than the other two brains. MacLean refers to the neocortex as "the mother of invention and father of abstract thought." The neocortex is where higher-level thinking occurs. This includes language, music, math, planning, memory storage and processing to create complex mental models, and so forth. I would add to that list other higher-level thinking such as understanding of natural laws, principles, inspiration, purpose, contribution, and other abstract ideas that don't exist within other species. This part of the human brain is what separates us from the rest of the animal kingdom. All of the technological advances, inventions, and the creation of other conveniences that we enjoy today were processed through the neocortex. All three brains serve an important purpose. We wouldn't want be without any of them.

Sun, Moon and Stars

When I consider the evidences all around me of the complexity, capability, and accomplishments of human beings as compared to mammals or reptiles, it is simply awesome. When I consider the sophistication of the human brain relative to the mammalian or reptilian brain, I would draw comparisons to the brightness of the stars, the moon, and the sun. In relative terms, the brightness of the stars is like the lizard brain. There is obviously intelligence there but certainly less than in the more sophisticated mammal.

Just as the moon is significantly brighter than the stars as you look in the night sky, so is the mammalian brain so much more intelligent than the lizard brain. It is interesting to note that even though the brightness of moon exceeds that of the stars, we primarily see both of them at night. The brightness of the sun, however, we see during the day. It's difficult if not impossible to see the moon or stars during the day, and yet, they are still out there. The sun is so much brighter than the moon and the stars by orders of magnitude. Likewise, the neocortex is not just *significantly* more intelligent than our other brains—but *infinitely* more so. Let the brightness of sun be a reminder to you each day to use your most intelligent brain, your neocortex. With it you will see yourself, others, and your opportunities more clearly. Much of society, however—from politics, business, the workplace, and even little league sports teams—is primarily set up as lizard-brain systems of "eat or be eaten, compete and conquer." You need to make a conscious and deliberate effort to use your most intelligent brain. It can be done, and to help you realize your best self—it must be done. To remind us of the immense potential and brightness of the human brain, I'll refer to the neocortex portion of the human brain as the divine brain.

One Brain Will Dominate

MacLean discovered something interesting about the interrelationship of our three brains, and that is what makes this topic relevant to time management. This interrelationship creates our view of the world. Our view of the world is important to consider, because it reflects and affects our use of our time. The more we deepen our understanding of our worldview and the functioning of our three brains, the more we'll clarify what is truly important in our lives and where we may choose to spend our time. Let's go back to the three brains and take a look at how they are interrelated.

Here's the big "aha." One of these three brains can dominate the other two! This means our reptile brain can dominate our thinking, and we view the world at the survival level: *Can I eat it?* or *Can it eat me?* This can be the case even with someone who has a highly-developed limbic system and neocortex. In other words, have you ever met people who are highly intelligent and capable, have the ability to get along well with people, but seem to use all their intelligence in the pursuit of conquering or defending against being conquered? Survival and conquest become the most important things in their lives. I'm not talking about what people declare is important. I'm talking about what their behaviors say is important. You may even see this mindset in all of their roles. They're in the survival, conquest, and competitive mode at work with co-workers and clients, at home with their spouse and children, at play whether with other people or computer games, and even while driving on the road. They see the world as primarily a competitive "eat or be eaten" environment. This may be part of the current reality in too much of the world around us, but that is not all of it. Unfortunately, in parts of the world where war and violence dominate the society, too many people are put in situations where the "eat or be eaten" mentality is in the forefront. So a certain degree of the "it's tough out there" mindset makes sense. Yet even in these extremely violent scenarios there are those who are able to rise above it and lead lives of inspiration and contribution. So it's not the environment or the actions and attitudes of other people that decide what we ultimately do. The part of the three-part brain that controls our thought processes, makes decisions, and dominates the other two brains also determines our behavior.

Even if the reptile brain is not in charge, the other concern is when the limbic system or monkey brain dominates the other two brains. This may mean that the pursuit of pleasure may be our dominant thinking and goal. This means that we can make decisions based on avoiding pain, repeating pleasure, or going with the social norm even when the divine brain says it's not a good idea. Have you ever seen smart people do dumb things? Sometimes we make decisions based on what felt good at the moment without accessing our higher or divine level of thinking. Have you ever asked someone after she made a big, obvious mistake, and you knew she was more than capable of figuring it out, "What were you thinking?" Have you ever wondered why you may also do dumb things—and not only that, but you do the same dumb things over and over again? You may even say to yourself, "I know better than to do that!" It may be helpful to change the question from, "What was I thinking?" to "Which one of my three brains dominated the thinking?" Too often the lizard brain or the monkey brain is the mastermind behind our actions, but the divine brain gets the blame. For example, have you ever made an unwise purchase on impulse (monkey brain), and you then interrogate your logical, rational, intelligent self (divine brain) as to why you made such a purchase? Our monkey brains are so powerful that they can actually hold our divine brains (the most intelligent part) hostage. Have you ever wondered how it is possible that on the one hand some people live inspirational lives, while on the other hand some people live their lives with more cruelty and violence than anything that is seen in the animal kingdom? It can be traced back to the strength of each of the three parts of our brains. Whether we live inspirational lives or vile lives depends on which of our three brains dominates our thinking.

Be Divinative

The best alternative is to make sure that the divine brain dominates our thinking. The more I thought about this the more I wanted to try and find the right word, the right adjective, to describe being definitive or unmistakable and absolute in our resolve to have our divine brains be our dominant brains. I wanted a word that expresses confidence in the power of principles. I wanted to find the word that captures the very best that exists in each of us. I wanted to find a word that described the purposeful and deliberate use of our divine brains. Because I couldn't find the right word, I came up with a new word. The word is "divinative." Be *divinative* in your thoughts and feelings. Be *divinative* in your words and actions. Be more *divinative* in how you choose to spend your time.

Let me reiterate that all three of our brains are interrelated, and each serves an important purpose. We wouldn't want to be without any of the three. The key is to have our divine brains dominate our thinking rather than to allow our lizard brains or monkey brains to dominate. That does not mean that we should try to go around and bypass our lizard brains and monkey brains, because they are interconnected. Even lizards and monkeys have all three brains just like humans, but the neocortex of a human is so much larger in relation to the reptilian and mammalian brains than any other creature on earth. The key is to develop habits where the neocortex or divine brains, dominate our thinking. Our intent then is to use and manage our time to develop our most intelligent divine brains, subordinate the signals from our lizard brains and monkey brains, be the people we want to be, and realize our potentials.

UGLY DUCKLING

The Ugly Duckling is a famous fairy tale by Danish author Hans Christian Andersen. The tale begins with a mother duck waiting patiently for her eggs to hatch. One by one the eggs hatch until the last one, which takes an unusually long time. When it finally hatches, the creature is large, ugly, and peculiar. Perceived as homely, it endures a great deal of physical and verbal abuse—not just from the ducks, but other farm animals as well. Even the girl who had to feed the poultry kicked it. Saddened, he wanders from the barn and lives with wild ducks and geese; they are not any kinder than those in the barn. After enduring more ridicule, he ends up going into the home of an old woman with her cat and a hen who tease him mercilessly. Sad and alone he declares to the cat and hen, "You don't understand me," and leaves. He sees a flock of wild swans and marvels at their beauty and strength. He had not seen such birds before. He is excited to see the swans, but he cannot join them. Winter arrives, and he spends a miserable winter alone. When spring finally arrives, he sees his reflection on the water, and he is no longer the gray and ugly duckling but has matured into a beautiful swan. He is welcomed into a flock of beautiful swans. I love the ending of this story.

> He had been persecuted and despised for his ugliness, and now he heard them say, he was the most beautiful of all the birds. Even the elder-tree bent down its bows into the water before him, and the sun shone warm and bright. Then he rustled his feathers, curved his slender neck, and cried joyfully, from the depths of his heart, "I never dreamed of such happiness as this, while I was an ugly duckling."

When I look at the lessons from this fairy tale and reality of the three parts of our brains, I come away with two lessons. The first lesson is the influence that others have on us. The ugly duckling was influenced by other animals, no matter where he went and no matter the context. The ugly duckling was affected by others in four different contexts. The first context is with those who knew him from birth. The second context is with extended family and friends. The third is with new friends. The fourth is with a completely new context and environment when it came to the old woman, cat and hen. One context was no better than the next. He was equally sad, disregarded, and mistreated no matter where he went. At the end of all this, he correctly concludes, "You don't understand me."

Similarly, having a new environment or new people we may associate with, may not change how we are viewed. In other words, even though the highly-intelligent divine brain (neocortex) is capable of so much, that capacity is marginalized when we don't have the approval of others (monkey brain). Remember the ugly duckling's refrain, "You don't understand me." This works both ways, however. If we can surround ourselves with people who can support and encourage the most intelligent and divine within us, we can do and be so much more than we even realize. We can then feel that the great potential we have, can be understood by others, and we will also understand ourselves better.

The second lesson is the realization that our greatest power is the power to choose. Consider the end of the tale when the ugly duckling declared,

I never dreamed of such happiness as this, while I was an ugly duckling.

Once the ugly duckling realized he was a swan, everything changed. How he viewed himself changed, and how others viewed him vastly improved as well. Granted, this is a fairy tale, and the transformation was a physical transformation. You may be asking yourself, "How would I go about viewing myself differently, not just physically but in all aspects?" The answer lies first in realizing that you may have been held back by the feedback of your lizard brain (everything is about survival) and your monkey brain (everything is about whether I feel good or bad, whether I am accepted by others or what my other emotions dictate). Relying wholly on acceptance means I am bound by the feedback from others, and I can only be as good as others say I am. Contrastingly, however, using more of the divine brain (neocortex) will propel us forward. The divine human brain (neocortex) is two-thirds of the total brain mass. Until we tap into the vast capabilities of the most intelligent part of ourselves—the divine brain—we are living well below our potential. It would be analogous to walking in the dimmer light of the moon or stars, when walking in the brightness of the noon day sun is an option. Everything we need, we already have and have always had—and it's so important that it is even protected by our skulls. We just need to tap into the divine part of our human brains. Be divinative. When we look at those we hold up as role models throughout history, they collectively stand as evidence of what is possible if we can tap into our divine brains and focus on being the very best people we can be.

NEED A NEW COACH

Think of it another way. Remember how your children, nieces and nephews or neighborhood kids would play sports year after year, sometimes with the same friends and teammates. Over the years you get your share of mediocre coaches. Every now and then, however, you get an exceptional coach, and everything changes. The kids play with more skill and teamwork. They win more games and have a lot more fun. Remember, the players are still the same players. The sport is still the same sport. The difference is the coach. The difference is with the person who is in charge. The coach's approach to practice and games is more disciplined and deliberate. More time is spent on skill development and strategy without losing the element of fun. How the coach responds to player mistakes is better. The way the coach sees each player is more uplifting. The players' response to the coach is encouraging and inspirational.

Similarly, we all have three brains, and they all have the ability to be the coach and call all the shots. Changing the way we see the world and how we see ourselves and others can be achieved by simply changing the coach—the mental coach. Make sure it's the divine brain calling all the shots and not the lizard brain or monkey brain. When the most intelligent brain is in charge, we'll see our progress differently. We'll see our setbacks and mistakes differently. We'll approach life with more hope, love, purpose, and forgiveness.

The greatest lesson of our three brains and the ugly duckling is that we can choose to put our divine brains in charge.

This is the single greatest decision that we can make. Once we make this decision, we'll realize that we can make every other decision. We will realize that we have the freedom to choose. Time and again when people make this shift they feel liberated and would want to exclaim like the ugly duckling,

I never dreamed of such happiness as this, while I was an ugly duckling.

Making this mental shift or coaching change is something that is going to take some practice, and we will use our time-management strategy to make sure that we do exactly that. The habits formed from the lizard brain and monkey brain don't just go away immediately, however, and those old habits sneak back in from time to time. Regardless, with some practice and persistence you can become more consistent in having your divine brain be your dominant brain.

MAKING A COACHING CHANGE

I love going on a morning run for my regular exercise, because it gives me a chance to just think. Sometimes I go on a run with a specific challenge that I want to think through. Other times I don't have anything specific to think about, and thoughts just pop into my mind. On one particular run when I didn't have anything unique to consider, my mind wandered, thinking about some rental property I had recently sold. It was in a different state than where I lived. The properties had not been managed well, and things had gone from bad to worse. I had been losing money every month. I couldn't manage the properties myself, because the location was too far away. This was at a time when the real estate market nationwide had taken a dive, and selling wasn't an option unless I was willing to sell the property at a deep loss. The problems mounted. Not only was my property manager not managing the properties well, but he was also misappropriating funds. I reluctantly sold the properties at a great loss, because it was the best option among all of my bad options.

As I began this run I started reliving what had happened, and I became furious all over again. In other words, my lizard brain, which asks the question, "Can I eat it?" or "Can it eat me?" was mocking me. It was in essence saying, "Hey, Charles, why did you let them eat us? Couldn't you come up with something to defend ourselves?" About that time, my monkey brain joined in on this pity party, and I was in a "woe is me" mode. I was going back and forth from feeling angry to feeling sad, and then back to angry again. My lizard brain was the head coach, and my emotionally-charged sad and angry monkey brain was the assistant coach. I could feel my blood pressure rising, and I got so upset that it finally dawned on me that I was running much faster than I normally do, and I don't even remember noticing or recalling anything in the previous half mile of my run. Then it hit me that my divine brain was not participating at all.

I immediately made a coaching change! I focused on lessons I had learned from this real-estate experience. My thoughts then drifted to how I could share what I had learned with family and friends about this real-estate scenario so as to spare them from what I had just been through. After that thought, my mind went to thoughts of not just how to help people with a similar real-estate predicament, but how to help people overcome such negative feelings I had, regardless of whether it involved real estate or any other scenario. Then I got really excited when I thought about how I could help my loved ones with their current struggles. It was a complete shift. My divine brain was now the head coach, and my monkey brain was still the assistant coach. This time, instead of my monkey brain giving me feelings of sadness and anger, I began feeling excited and hopeful. In essence, my divine brain and monkey brain were having a discussion saying, "Isn't it exciting that we can take this bad experience and not just turn it into something better for us, but also from our learning, we can create a means for teaching and serving our loved ones to improve their lives? Who knows, perhaps we can even impact people we've never met, who can share in what we've learned." About this time, I was about half a mile away from home. I was so excited that I sprinted home, and that was the easiest part of the whole run. Now even my lizard brain that controls breathing and muscle movements was joining the fun. I couldn't wait to share my experience. When the divine brain is the head coach, so to speak, calling all the shots, the monkey brain and lizard brain make great assistant coaches.

YOU CAN'T JUST DO THE OPPOSITE

Here is something else that I learned from that morning run. There are times when our lizard brains take over, and we want to compete, contend, or conquer. These are all lizard-brain strategies. Sometimes our monkey brains take over, and we want to compare, criticize, or complain. These are common lizard and monkey brain tactics when we are feeling bad. We simply can't go from competing, contending, and conquering to *not* competing, *not* contending, and *not* conquering. The reason we can't simply shift to the opposite of where we've been, is because we are still in the same brain. With our lizard brains asking the question, "Can I eat it?" or "Can it eat me?" we are simply shifting from the *eating or conquering* thinking, to *getting eaten thinking* or vice versa. When the monkey brain says we are feeling bad, we want to tell ourselves to feel better. Either way, we are still in the monkey-brain mode of processing our world in terms of feeling good versus feeling bad. We need a whole new mindset. We need a new coach calling the shots. We need to have the divine brain take over. We need the relative brightness of the sun (divine brain) to illuminate our thinking and understanding. We'll address in our time-management strategy how to have the divine brain dominate our thinking and be more divinative.

CHAPTER FIVE

FOUNDATIONAL REALITIES OF TIME MANAGEMENT

THERE are four foundational realities of time management to consider. These are critically important for two reasons: First, they involve fundamental shifts in our thinking. Remember when you got your driver's license and drove for the first time by yourself? The world looked different after that point, and you saw yourself differently as well. These four foundational principles will have the same effect if you haven't made these shifts yet. You will see the world differently. Remember your three brains. We'll start making the shift so that the neocortex or divine brain will be in charge. Secondly, the rest of the content of the book will build on these four realities. I refer to these four realities as:

- Time is opportunity
- Clark Kent to Superman
- The distance between heaven and hell
- All-you-can-eat buffet

TIME IS OPPORTUNITY

The beginning of wisdom is the definition of terms.

—Socrates

To gain wisdom, when it comes to time management it is important to first define time. Instead of defining time as a duration, interval, or even as a series of events, let's define time a different way.

Time is opportunity. Time is measured in units of possibilities.

Isn't this an exciting definition? Instead of thinking of time as a series of events that we are trying to manage through to-do lists and calendars, time is a series of possibilities that create opportunities, which in turn will create additional possibilities, and so forth. My purpose then is not just to manage time, but to think creatively to maximize and multiply my opportunities. When you do your weekly or daily planning, isn't it a lot more fun to think in terms of how to create, maximize, and multiply your opportunities this week or this day, as opposed to simply writing a list of the things that need to get done this day or week? It even changes the way you look at what you have already planned.

- Instead of feeling guilty about leaving your kids yet again when called upon to help your neighbor, it can become an opportunity to teach your children the joy of service as you serve your neighbor *with* your kids. Teach them to have empathy for the needs of others.
- Instead of delegating cleaning responsibilities to your children, it becomes an opportunity for family bonding and teaching time to work with your kids. Teach them that you want more than just for them to clean, but you want them to value and see the benefits of order, cleanliness, structure, and pride. Teach the importance of creating standards of excellence for themselves and living up to them.
- Instead of just helping your children with their schoolwork, help expand their vision of education. Tell them that part of the purpose of education is to gain knowledge, convert knowledge to wisdom, and then use that wisdom to lead a life of contribution.
- When you go on vacation, instead of focusing on just hitting the vacation sites, focus on creating wonderful memories.
- Work meetings can shift from being talking memos to engaging colleagues to tap into creative solutions and also new innovative solutions.
- Be more deliberate in taking the time to really listen to work associates instead of just focusing on what you are going to say. It's amazing when you hear great ideas and opportunities—and they

already exist in all organizations, if only more people would take the time to listen.

- Instead of just thinking of ideas on how to do your professional job well, think in terms of how you can expand your opportunities beyond your job description and even beyond your current employer.
- Look at your long-term goals through a different light. With the infrastructure and the new norm of conducting business globally, consider what contributions are needed, not just locally, but throughout the world. Which do you have the skills, knowledge, and passion to provide? The possibilities—and hence the opportunities—are endless. Time is indeed opportunity.

Have you ever sat down for your weekly or daily planning, and you're trying to figure out what you should write? Perhaps you start by writing your list of urgent matters. After you complete your urgent to-do list you are at a loss as to what's next. You may be asking yourself, "What should I be doing with my 168 hours this week? Perhaps you are puzzled, and you just sit there staring at the ceiling, trying to access information in your brain. Most don't have the questions to ask themselves, so they are simply trying to remember what it is they may have forgotten to do. Consequently, their planning time is simply an exercise in writing down the urgent things and memory recall. Others focus on identifying the most important or highest-leverage thing they can do for that day or week. This is a better question, but most people draw a blank when they think in terms of superlatives (most, best, fastest, highest, and other "est" ending words) and go back to memory recall. Here are a few questions you could ask yourself:

- What would maximize or multiply my opportunities today or this week in my different roles?
- Wouldn't it be cool if I could …? Use your imagination, and don't limit yourself. What unique contribution would you like to make? What needs are so obvious to you, but you are amazed that the problem hasn't been addressed yet? What would need to change to make your contributions come to pass?

Aren't these more profound questions? For most people, either new ideas come to mind, or they get a fresh perspective on existing ideas. Planning time really does become opportunity time or "opp time."

When you view time as opportunity you will recognize that time is and has been in great abundance, and has actually been increasing for quite a while now. You don't look at time as a scarce resource where you are constantly finding yourself without enough. Instead you see time as a resource that is meant to be multiplied—and your job is to figure out exciting ways to make that happen. For example, when you look back at the economic evolution of man, we provided for our basic needs for food by hunting animals or gathering wild fruits. In other words, there were fewer possibilities, when it comes to meeting our basic needs in the hunter/gatherer age than there are today. We found a new and better way to meet our basics meets, and it was called farming. Our chances for providing for our basic needs multiplied, and the yield increased. In other words, time increased because our opportunities increased. The next evolution went from farming to the industrial revolution, and our opportunities were multiplied and magnified once again.

Think for a moment what this simple analysis means to each of us daily. I could go hunting to feed my family, and who knows when I would be back or if I would return with anything. I could farm, and I would have a harvest, but it's questionable what the amount or quality will be. Today, instead of hunting or farming to meet my basic needs for food, I am compensated for working as I see fit. I then take part of my pay and easily purchase a wide variety of foods without having to grow it or hunt for those foods myself. Today I can go to a grocery store and get something from the meat department. Push my cart down to the produce section and get some fruits and vegetables. I can pick up some spices and get some desert while I'm at it, and I can do this night or day, in the middle of summer or the dead of winter. I can also do all of this on my way home from work. Amazing!

Our time (or our opportunities in this simple illustration) is greater now than ever in the history of man. Why? Those who have gone before us have been maximizing and multiplying opportunities for us. We can now do so much more with less effort. We take so much for granted, such as cars, planes, cell phones, and the Internet. Think about how much change has accelerated, even lately. Can you believe that the iPod was only launched in 2001? Google wasn't a publicly traded company until 2004, and now Google is part of our everyday vocabulary as a verb. Instead of going to the library and not knowing where to turn to find the information I need, today I don't even need to leave the comforts of home. I just Google it!

I remember last year when my then seven-year-old came home so excited, because the parent who gave him a ride home from soccer practice has this really cool car. He said, "The door has this handle that you turn one way, it goes in a circle and it makes the window go down, and you turn it the other way and it makes the window go up." It took me a while to figure out what he was talking about, and then I realized that my seven-year-old son had only known power windows his whole life. He had never turned a handle before to make the window go up or down; he just pushes a button. How many people do you know who don't have power windows? The opportunities around us are plentiful and are multiplying quicker than we know in big ways such as Google or in smaller ways such as power windows. Are you going to take an active or passive role in all of this progress?

Even though opportunities around us are multiplying like weeds, do we plan our days and view time like a hunter of thousands of years ago trying to figure out where to go and what to do from one hunt to the next? Or do we access our divine brains and not only think in terms of today, but in terms of multiplying our opportunities for tomorrow and the next day—and the next weeks and months after that? There has never been a more exciting time to be alive in the history of mankind. Again, time is opportunity measured in units of possibilities. When we make this shift, miracles are just around the corner.

CLARK KENT TO SUPERMAN

Superman is the fictional comic book superhero. He was discovered and raised by a Kansas farmer and his wife, and is known by the name of Clark Kent. When Clark discovered that he had superhuman abilities, he resolved to use his strengths for the benefit of all humanity. He hides his identity as Superman by working as a "mild-mannered reporter." I remember watching the black and white television shows of Superman where he goes into a phone booth and transforms into Superman complete with a cape and big letter "S" on his chest—and then flies off to help someone in distress.

Moms and those in management and executive roles are thrust into "Superman" roles and responsibilities whether they want to be or not. With a birth of a child or an announced managerial promotion, a person's role can change in an instant—almost as fast as Clark Kent can change into Superman as he goes into a phone booth. Gone are the days when people can hide behind the role of "mild-mannered reporter." A young lady can afford to pick and choose when to use her superhuman abilities to benefit mankind, but once her role changes to the role of a mother, all of her superhuman strengths are needed 24/7. Her thoughts shift from thinking about what is best for her to unconditionally loving her children. This is a fundamental shift in thinking that applies to all of these foundational realities. There is the shift from thinking independently to thinking about the welfare of others.

Similarly, when someone has a non-management work role, he can focus on individual performance. He can pace himself and really focus his energies throughout the work day. When people take on supervisory responsibility, most successful managers and executives change their focus. The focus goes from the benefit of oneself to the health of the team or enterprise. The success of the executive or manager is defined by the success of the team. The shift goes from *me* to *we*. Regardless of the business hours, the health and welfare of the team is on the manager's or executive's mind 24/7. When an executive or manager makes this fundamental shift to being more concerned about the welfare of the team instead of the welfare of the executive individually, the rest of the team can sense and feel it, and they will rally behind the leader. If the team senses the executive is only in it for himself, the team emotionally withdraws and contributes less than their best.

When these mom- or manager- or executive-role shifts occur, the time management philosophy and practice also needs to change. Before the role shift, I can plan my day and ask what "I" am going to do today, and the context is my personal performance. After the role shift, the time management question becomes, "What conditions do I need to create to benefit my family or work team today?"

Look at it another way. The mom and management roles are much like a gardener role. Think for a moment what a gardener might need to grow wonderful tomatoes. You may consider sunlight, water, soil, fertilizer, care, taking out weeds, and so forth. What the gardener is doing in essence is creating the conditions that maximize the growth of the seed. There's not much a gardener can do with the seed itself. The gardener can't wish for a cantaloupe harvest from a tomato seed. Similarly, the mom's and management's role is to create conditions for family members or team members to grow. They focus their time and effort on significantly improving the chances for success.

The point of this foundational reality is this: with the role change to mother or management, change the time management focus from individual performance to building a family culture at home or team culture at work. Once I realized this, I saw its application in all my roles. Whether you have additional roles such as a soccer coach, teacher, church roles, or are part of some association leadership, shift your thinking from, "What can I do for me" to "How do I facilitate the acceptance of the values of the organization so that those values are shared?" or "How can I multiply the opportunities for my family or team?"

DISTANCE BETWEEN HEAVEN AND HELL

Comfortably seated on a business flight, I was watching people as they filed in. One passenger in particular had a peculiar look of excitement. She sat next to me and after a few moments of chit-chat, I asked her where she was coming from or headed to. She excitedly said that she just came from a retreat where she learned what she felt was the most important lesson she has ever learned. Curious, I asked her what the most important lesson was. She said, "I learned the physical distance between heaven and hell."

Of course, being intrigued, I just had to ask, "So, how far is that?"

She said, "About 18 inches—the distance from your head to your heart! Heaven is the state when your head and your heart work together to help you realize the person you have the potential to be. Hell is when your head and heart are not in synch."

This was a profound idea. As I began to ponder what she had said, I thought it had merit in its application. One of the first things that came to mind was how many wonderful things we already do without ever appreciating the profound effect we have on others and ourselves. In other words, we are evaluating with our mind and forgetting to evaluate with the heart as well.

Consider these simple acts.

- You come home after a hard day's work, and your child comes running to you with arms open and a big smile to greet you and hug you. Doesn't that make you look forward to coming home the next day?

- Your boss notices your efforts at work, and acknowledges you in front of your peers. Don't you have just an added bounce to your step and want to continue to do a good job?
- You frequent a store, because they are cheerful and genuinely want to help you. Isn't that the reason you frequent that store, even if their prices aren't better than another store?

These acts stem from the heart, not just the mind. Do we respond in kind? What if everything we did was more than a sense of duty, but balanced with love? What if we consciously responded in kind to our child's welcome home greeting? What if we thanked our boss for the kind words, and looked for the opportunities to lift another colleague. What if we acknowledged to the friendly and helpful person at the store, how much we appreciate the genuine service? What if in our planning we weighed the effects of our planned actions both on ourselves and others? What if we weighed them with the heart and the mind? If we did, we would recognize how much of what we already do is good, and that we need to celebrate those acts and do more of the same instead of thinking it's not a big deal. Are you kidding me? It's a huge deal!

Another lesson that I learned from this airplane passenger's excitement was her expectation. It was more than hope. She believed in her heart of hearts, that if her heart and mind were aligned, she would see improvement and experience fulfillment. It would be heaven. Have you ever met people who, in choosing their careers, have reconciled the reasons for being in their professions, both in their minds and hearts and not just the wallet? They love what they do, and they are very good at it. Whether it's your mechanic, pharmacist, the person in the IT department, or the master teacher in your child's school, those individuals excel, because they love what they do and they do it well. You have probably met people in the exact same professions, and have wondered how they ever got their jobs or why they wanted those jobs in the first place. They either dislike what they do, or there's no passion behind their work. They are just logging in hours, and they are miserable.

I think most people are somewhere in the middle. Most of us haven't yet taken the time to reconcile in our hearts and minds why we do what we do.

You may not have your dream job as your first job, but if you consistently pay close attention and evaluate your life's work with your heart and mind, then every assignment, promotion, or job change, guides you closer to the type of work that suits you best, and those you impact will be so much better for your contribution and your adjustment. You can expect that going through such an exercise will make a profound difference. Deliberately evaluate your current situation with both the heart and mind. How do we make sure such thinking is incorporated in our time management planning?

In a conversation with a high school principal, he confided in me that he hated being a high school principal. He wanted to take some time to examine his life and figure out what was best for him professionally. The next time I saw him there was a change in his countenance. He looked happy and excited. He said he figured out what he wanted to be professionally. After taking the time to go through the mental and emotional struggle to decide what was best for him, he decided he wanted to be—a high school principal. In the day-to-day grind and minutiae, he said that somehow he had lost his way. He had forgotten why he got into the education profession to begin with. Taking the time to reconcile what he felt in his heart and knew in his mind he should do professionally, made the difference between his professional work becoming a little bit of heaven or a little bit of hell. Maybe your experience won't be a recommitment to your current role, but may cause you to move toward a completely different industry all together. Regardless, if after you consider all the trade-offs, and the move gives you greater peace of mind and heart, it will be the right move in the end.

The same can be said of being a parent. Have you ever thought just how profound of an impact a parent has? Consider the impact of parents from the child's perspective. Here are a few testimonials.

> All that I am or ever hope to be, I owe to my angel Mother.
> —Abraham Lincoln

> Directly after God in heaven, comes a Papa.
> —Mozart as a boy

My mother said to me, "If you become a soldier you'll be a general; if you become a monk you'll end up as a pope." Instead, I became a painter and wound up as Picasso."

—Pablo Picasso

I can only imagine that the success of these parents, emanated from the heart, mind, and their very being. When parents labor from the mind and the heart, they are revered and will forever become the most influential persons in the lives of their children. (Remember the earlier reference to taking a survey on the most influential person in your life and having others take a similar informal survey.) When parents exercise such wisdom, their influence transitions to the next generation, and these parents truly earn the title: Grand Parents.

As we talk about a new focus in considering time management, know that this is not just a cerebral exercise. This notion of building a culture of being more and not just doing more requires examination of the heart as well as the mind or head. The problem with most time-management philosophies is neglecting the *heart* and our *being* in exchange for a focus on the *doing*. As I teach workshops, whether for work or for the home, people come into the course looking for ideas on how to get better. In other words, people are looking for changes of the mind (Unknowingly, most are asking questions coming from their lizard and monkey brains.) The further into the training we go there is a point at which the light bulb comes on; there is a fundamental shift in thinking as well as feeling, and people get it. *Getting it* means your heart and your mind are in agreement. Both the mind and heart are equally important.

This time management system will give a more holistic view of time management and life leadership. It ensures that the philosophy is imbedded into the time-management practice. This approach is exciting because of its simplicity as well as its holistic approach.

ALL-YOU-CAN-EAT BUFFET
VERSUS SELECTIVE NEGLECT

There is an all-you-can-eat buffet close to our home, and our family likes to go there from time to time. Everyone in our family enjoys going for different reasons. Some like to go because they don't have to cook or clean up afterwards. Some claim they are so hungry that they could eat everything. Others enjoy the unlimited deserts. Others love the salad bar, while some head straight for their favorite entrées. The options and combinations you can eat in an all-you-can-eat buffet are so numerous that it would take some effort to compute. We always enjoy ourselves. No one leaves hungry, but sometimes some of us feel that we ate more than was necessary, and we get that bloated feeling.

There are some parallels between the all-you-can eat-buffet and our time-management approach. I think too many of us go about our time-management strategies and to-do lists like some of us go to an all-you-can-eat buffet. We are hungry to achieve, excited and anxious about everything we can do with our time. With all of the options that only our imagination can limit, we try to do it all. Like eating too much at the buffet, trying to tackle too much in any given period of time, gives us that same bloated, sick, "I shouldn't have done that" feeling.

Just as you can't possibly eat everything in an all-you-can-eat buffet today and every day, you won't get everything done that can be possibly done in a day and repeat the feat every day! It seems an obvious enough idea mentally, but emotionally and psychologically, we all wish it were otherwise. You just have to get over it. Even if everything is carefully mapped out, there is always an X-factor. It's called life. Life happens. Life always puts a kink even in the most well-thought-out plans.

The key to maximizing your peace and productivity is what I refer to as *selective neglect.* Time management philosophies and practices primarily focus on what you are going to do but seldom, if ever, on what you are choosing *not* to do. Saying yes is easy. Knowing when and how to say no is the tricky part. Because there are not enough hours in a day, many times we are left to arbitrarily choose what to do and what not to do. More often than not, our decisions on what we are going to do are based on an event's urgency or how we feel at the time (monkey or mammalian brain), only to find out later that perhaps it wasn't the highest-leverage thing we could have done.

Just as a side note, I only schedule about two-thirds of my day, because unexpected variables (you know, that life thing) fill in the other third. I find that if I fill more than two-thirds of my calendar, the X-factor throws off my schedule, and I just get frustrated that I didn't accomplish everything I set out to do. I run out of time and can't catch up. Some of you may cringe at the thought of having a third of your day unscheduled. Two-thirds of your time scheduled, so long as it is highly leveraged, and one-third unscheduled is not a hard and fast number. You will find the appropriate ratio that works best for you. Perhaps you will schedule more, perhaps a tad less. You will find as you work through this philosophy that you won't be as concerned about how much time is scheduled as you will be about the leverage of what is scheduled. You'll be more concerned with leading the kind of life that will help you create the culture of being more and not just doing more.

Back to selective neglect in the all-you-can-eat buffet of life. In a corporate meeting I attended where a company was newly acquired, strategy was the topic of the day. Everyone came anxious to exchange thoughts on the great possibilities in the future. Everyone shared with great passion what they thought were the greatest opportunities that should be pursued. Finally, one very astute and sincere veteran manager said, "As I listen to everyone's ideas, time and time again, I have come to the conclusion that the best idea I've heard is the last idea I heard."

Have you ever had this happen to you? Have you ever been so convinced by someone else' idea only to lament later, "What was I thinking?" Have you ever been convinced by a passionate plea from your children, yet later, you can't recall how you ever came to such a silly conclusion? Do you know why advertising works, and you end up buying things that you had no plans to buy? There is a common thread to all three of these scenarios.

When we make any decision, consciously or unconsciously, we filter our decisions through our decision criteria. Sometimes we are deliberate about our decision criteria, and other times someone else will dictate the decision criteria for us, if we are not paying attention. The veteran manager was open to new ideas, but he didn't have his conscious decision criteria to help him differentiate between a great idea versus a mediocre one that had been delivered with great excitement. For example, as a parent we may unknowingly make a decision based on taking discomfort and stress away from our children, when those very challenges represent growth and a great teaching moment. When it comes to time management, making a conscious decision about our decision criteria is foundational to knowing what we should be scheduling in the first place. It is a vital component to know what to selectively neglect. This again is tapping into the very best that we have inside of us (divine brain) and not just what feels right at the moment (monkey brain).

Selective neglect is having the understanding that we can't do everything. It is coming to terms with knowing we can't say *yes* to everything, and that we have to say *no* in the all-you-can-eat buffet options of life. Selective neglect is taking the time to come up with our decision criteria. Selective neglect is also realizing that if our choices help us be the person we want to be, we will look back with great satisfaction and peace that we made the right choices.

CHAPTER SIX

OVERVIEW OF SIX ALLEGORIES

WE have just set the foundation for this new time-management philosophy. As you master the following six allegories you will have the mind, heart, and tools to pilot your life from a culture of doing more to a culture of being more. These allegories will also help you create the conditions for a happy family culture and a healthy team culture. A healthy team culture would apply as much at work, at church, at school, or any organization where you participate. From the first allegory to the sixth you will move from the most universal concepts of implementing this time-management philosophy to very specific practices. The implementation of this time management philosophy is remembering and implementing the lessons of six allegories. Each allegory will answer one of the why, who, what, how, where, and when questions.

1. **Trees**: The easiest way to remember this allegory is to picture the number one and the long trunk of a tree.

    Question: Why is a focus on character development a necessary part of time management, and what difference does it make?

2. **Oxen Pull**: The easiest way to recall this allegory is to hold an image of two oxen yoked together.

    Question: Who are the people essential to helping you be the person you want to be, and how will you identify them?

3. **Three Combination Lock:** The easiest way to remember this allegory is to form a vision in your mind of a combination lock like the one you probably used in high school and the need to remember three numbers used in proper sequence.

   Question: What are your most important roles, and how can you improve in each of them?

4. **Four Seasons:** Think of the four seasons of winter, spring, summer, and autumn with the predictable sequence.

   Question: How are changes, improvements, and results achieved, and how do we align our time to consistently develop character and achieve our goals?

5. **Five Golden Rings:** This of course is easiest to keep in mind when you recall the Christmas carol, "Twelve Days of Christmas." The fifth day in the carol says, "On the fifth day of Christmas my true love sent to me, five golden rings."

   Question: Where and how do I start in my quest to develop my character?

6. **Plane:** There's not a clever way to remember this allegory other than it's the last one. However, the tool we have created will integrate all of these concepts in a week-at-a-glance format.

   Question: When should I expect to see results, and how do I implement all of this in a simple and powerful way?

CHAPTER SEVEN

ALLEGORY #1:
ALLEGORY OF THE TREES

THE world's oldest continually standing tree is the Bristlecone Pine, living nearly five thousand years, and having grown to about 60 feet high. The Redwood tree, in contrast, can reach over 350 feet in height and can live more than two thousand years. A closer study of these trees reveals other interesting things that can teach us some very valuable lessons.

The Bristlecone lives where practically nothing else can. The Bristlecone Pine is almost always found in elevations above 10,000 feet in the windy mountaintops in the western portion of the United States. The growing season is a meager six weeks, with precipitation of less than a foot per year. This desert condition, where these trees thrive, is one of the driest places on earth in the summer and is very cold in the winter.

The Redwood trees, on the other hand, live in a mild, moist climate in the coastal northwest part of California. The Redwood trees receive an average of 70 inches of precipitation per year. The soil is rich. There is infrequent frost where these Redwood trees thrive, and it snows very little.

The oldest Bristlecone Pines live in the most exposed sites, with a considerable amount of space between each tree. Not only is there space between each tree, but the Bristlecone is also isolated because few other species can survive the rugged conditions. The Bristlecone roots sink wide and deep into the rocky soil. The Redwood trees, on the other hand, grow close together with other Redwood trees, and their roots are shallow and interwoven.

What a contrast between the Bristlecone and Redwood trees. Despite their differences, they both live so long. Perhaps you can see the parallels between these trees and your own life or the lives of your family members, extended family members, neighbors, or colleagues at work. I would imagine some of them come from ideal conditions, as does the Redwood tree. Other people however, may come from harsh conditions as the Bristlecone Pine encounters. Regardless, you probably know people from both extremes who manage to live wonderful lives and are sources of inspiration for all of us. How can people, like these trees, have such divergent backgrounds, yet, regardless of background, become the people they want to be?

Let's look again at the Bristlecone and Redwood trees for more insights. The longevity for both of these trees is partially attributed to their ability to fight fires from without and disease from within. Fire and disease are the main reasons why other trees don't survive as long as the Bristlecone and Redwood. Bacteria, fungus, or insects prey upon most plants. However, the Bristlecone tree has a dense and highly resinous wood that acts as a barrier to insects and bacteria. The dry air in the region helps preserve the trees from rotting.

The Redwood tree fights against disease differently. The bark of the Redwood tree may be over a foot thick and contains tannin, which protects the tree from insects, fungus, and disease. There is no insect that can kill a Redwood tree. Both of these trees have the ability to fight attacks from within because of the makeup of the trees themselves.

As far as fighting fires, the longevity of the Bristlecone needles and the inadequacy of other trees and plants to grow in such harsh conditions, make the vegetation around the Bristlecone Pine sparse, limiting the capacity for fire or the spread of fire to other trees in the event of a lightning strike. The Redwood trees fight fires with thick spongy bark that contains materials with similar chemical make-up as those used today in fire extinguishers.

Whether it's these trees striving for longevity, or us trying to become the people we want to be, either requires dealing with our own fires from without and disease from within. It requires that our very character be resistant against those things that tempt us to compromise our integrity. The very word *disease* means "without ease." So living with integrity or living according to our chosen beliefs and values gives us peace; otherwise we live without ease. Fighting our personal fires from without requires having a barrier of protection thick enough to withstand tremendous heat, like the Redwood tree, or we must put ourselves in an environment where fires can't spread or intensify, like the Bristlecone Pine.

It is interesting to note that with some Redwood trees, you will see the trees hollowed out. They are sometimes referred to as chimney trees. Cracks or spaces in the bark contribute to these Redwood trees being hollowed out. Although the bark itself is thick, over time, fires attack the Redwood trees through these openings. The more the trees are hollowed out through many fires over the centuries, the weaker the tree becomes, and the Redwood tree strains to hold its tremendous bulk and eventually crumbles under its own weight.

In this time management philosophy and strategy, we are not merely trying to get more done, we are trying to realize the people we want to be, while at the same time fighting against other demands (fires from without and disease from within) that would take us off course. As we have learned from the Redwood chimney tree, we need to be vigilant against those little cracks and openings where fires from without can attack. We need to be equally careful with the big and small activities over time that would detract us from being the type of people we can realize. This will take time and more especially practice and persistence.

PRAYER AND MEDITATION

We mentioned that both the Bristlecone Pines and Redwood trees fight disease from within by the very make-up of the tree. So how do we create this barrier of protection from fires from without and disease from within, which rob us of our time and focus to *be* more and not just *do* more?

We need to dedicate a portion of our time every day to strengthening our divine brains.

How do we do this? Recall the lesson from our three-part brains that we have the power to decide that our divine brains will dominate our thinking instead of our lizard brains or monkey brains. This is the first great decision we need to make— that we can make a deliberate decision to have our divine brains dominate our thoughts and harness our power to choose.

Consider the poem "Invictus" from William Ernest Henley that celebrates this power that exists in us.

Invictus

Out of the night that covers me,
Black as the Pit from pole to pole,
I thank whatever gods may be
For my unconquerable soul.
In the fell clutch of circumstance
I have not winced nor cried aloud.
Under the bludgeoning of chance
My head is bloody, but unbowed.
Beyond this place of wrath and tears
Looms but the Horror of the shade,
And yet the menace of the years
Finds, and shall find me, unafraid.
It matters not how strait the gate,
How charged with punishments the scroll,
I am the master of my fate:
I am the captain of my soul.

This is a wonderful poem that arouses in mankind the ability to realize his/her potential. Look at how mankind has improved over the centuries and how that improvement is accelerated year after year. It is simply awesome. We are all so fortunate that enough people have made the huge decision to intellectually tap into their divine brains. We have all benefited from these advancements. Despite the declaration and evidence that we are each the masters of our fates and the captains of our souls, however, we also know that our abilities and courage have limitations. The recognition and humility to acknowledge such limitations can be one of our greatest strengths. For within all of us is also a voice that says there is a greater source of power higher than our own. We all have the ability and opportunity to consistently tap into spiritual strength or our source for meaning. For some, spiritual strength means religion, while for others it may come from nature, science, literature, music, art, and so forth. Because by some estimates over 80 percent of everyone worldwide is affiliated with a religious group, let me give the context of spiritual strength through the lens of religion.

The second great decision we can make besides deciding that our divine brains will be our dominant brains is to start and end each day using our divine brains. Being who we are or hope to be depends on which brain is allowed to be most dominant and which brain is most used.

Praying or connecting to your source of meaning through meditation is a powerful use of your time when it is done as the first activity of the morning and the last activity at night. The world around us is a competitive and complex place where survival and conquest (lizard brain), emotions, and fitting in (monkey brain) can dominate our days. When we don't begin our days by praying or connecting to our sense of meaning, the lizard-brain and monkey-brain activities that surround our world begin to clamor for our attention. If we do not make a conscious decision to begin and end the day with *divine-brain* type thinking, we will be drawn to the lizard-brain and monkey-brain type thinking by default.

> Prayer is not an old woman's idle amusement. If properly understood and applied, it is the most potent instrument of action.
> —Mahatma Gandhi

Consistent prayer and connection to purpose increases our capacity and ability to use our divine brains in the hard moments. Think back to a time when you regretted doing or saying something. They need not be huge regrets, just the little ones. Perhaps you got impatient and said unkind things. Perhaps in a moment of anger you acted inappropriately. For most of us, these regrettable moments happened when our lizard brains or monkey brains dominated our thinking. We wish we had the moments back and hope that our very best divine brains would have made better decisions or found better words.

Consistent daily morning and evening prayer or connection to meaning through meditation build our reservoir of strength in those tough moments. What should you pray for and meditate about? Begin each morning by reviewing those things for which you are genuinely grateful. Although not everything is perfect, going through this "gratitude attitude" exercise will help all of us realize how blessed we are in all things. Be grateful for the natural beauties you have around you every day, and pray to have eyes to see them. We have relationships that give us strength and hope. Be grateful for friends and family who love us and whom we love. We have physical conveniences and technological advances that kings, pharaohs, and rulers of days past could only have dreamt of. Review and be grateful for your belief system and how it has blessed your life. Review and be grateful for your unique talents. Be grateful for challenges that help you grow and develop your character. Be grateful for life itself and for the freedoms you enjoy. As you go through this simple exercise, can't you just feel your awareness expanding? What are you grateful for?

Follow your expressions of gratitude by thinking about how you can improve yourself as well as lift others today on a personal level, professionally, and in all areas of your life. Recall that we defined time as opportunities measured in units of possibilities. Pray to see possibilities and for opportunities to realize them. Pray for the courage to live according to the person you want to be. Before you go to bed, review how you have lifted others each day. Celebrate your valiant efforts to live according to your beliefs in both the big and little things. This daily and nightly accountability system will remind you to keep your divine brain as the dominant brain. Your divine brain will also help you make the adjustments you need to make to realize the person you want to be. Add to this the habit of daily reading of scriptures or inspiring literature. The lessons you learn from your reading will also help you keep your divine brain as your dominant brain. As you make these simple activities habits, you will notice your very nature will change, and you will recognize that you are indeed divine.

ZIGZAG PATH TO GROWTH

When we examined the Redwood tree and Bristlecone Pines, we explored primarily their protection from fire and disease, which helped them to achieve longevity. Let's shift from protection to actual growth. If prayer and meditation along with reading scriptures and inspiring literature is my focus at the beginning and ending of each day, what should be my focus in between? What does it take for us to realize our potential and continue to grow and lead lives of fulfillment and contribution? First, let's take a look at how growth occurs and what may restrain our progress. Let's go back to the monkey brain for a moment. Remember that part of the monkey brain says that it is more desirable to feel good than to not feel good. This mammalian part of our brains (or monkey brain) tells us that we would rather avoid pain and move towards repeating pleasure.

Not So Good (Pain)   HOW DO I FEEL?   Good (Pleasure)

So in the following continuum, given the choice between the far left side where we don't feel so good or we feel pain, compared to moving to the extreme right where we feel good or we feel pleasure, nearly everyone would likely prefer moving to the far right. In our zigzag path to growth this continuum will be our X-axis. The Y-axis of this model represents our growth and contribution. Growth and contribution refers to our personal growth and contributing our unique talents and abilities for the benefit of others. Together they are a big part of our mission. There is a voice within each of us that says, "I am somebody. I am a person of great worth. I have unique talents and insights that can contribute and benefit others in significant ways." Moving further up the Y-axis represents higher levels of growth and contribution towards our life's unique mission. Let's put these two together. When we have achieved high growth and contribution, and we also feel great, then we are achieving our mission—our sense of "being."

Figure 1: DESIRED GROWTH PATH

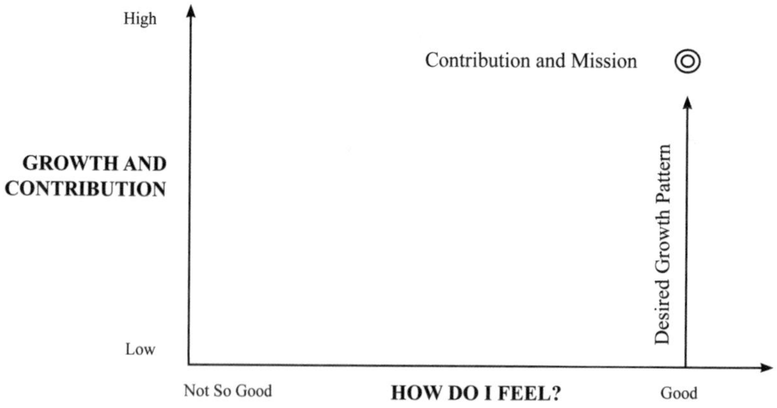

Of course, we all wish that we could feel good all of the time while growing and living a life that is fulfilling for ourselves as we contribute to our loved ones and the rest of humanity—and live happily ever after. That is the kind of life that is represented in the graph above. Unfortunately, it doesn't work that way, and our experiences verify it as well.

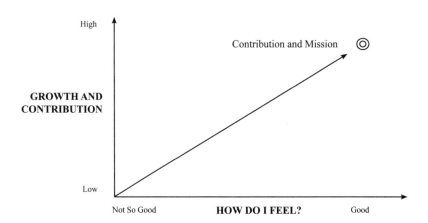

Figure 2: **TYPICAL GROWTH PATH**

This Figure 2 graph is a simple representation of how our growth more typically occurs. Think back to when you were learning how to ride a bike. I remember going through that experience, and I was terrified. In other words, on the X-axis of how I was feeling, I was on the far left. As far as my growth when it comes to riding a bike, I was at the bottom. I could hardly put my feet on the pedals, because I kept stretching my legs out, anticipating and bracing myself for when I would tilt too far to the left or to the right, and perhaps fall. The more I practiced, however, the better I felt, and I was also growing and improving my bike-riding skills. In other words, I was moving further to the right as well as further up on this diagonal line. Once I understood how to ride a bike, I was having fun and feeling good. It's the same bike, and I was the same kid, but the change in how I felt was a result of my confidence, growth, and development. Think of the times when you have gone through a similar growth experience whether the context is personal or professional.

MATH HOMEWORK

I could just as easily have chosen any school subject, but I'll use math as an example, because this is what happened in our home. I have an eight-year-old son, Ben, who works very hard in his school work. He is a good student and does well on all of his school subjects. But on one particular day, he'd had enough of math. He couldn't understand the concepts, and he just sat there and wept. Over and over he would say, "I hate math. I hate math. I hate math." Every now and then he would insert, "Math is stupid. Math is stupid." My eleven-year son, Spencer, glanced over at his distraught brother, looked at Ben's homework, and said, "Are you kidding me? My math homework is harder than your homework. I wish I had your math homework!" Let me graph how our continual individual growth typically occurs over time.

Figure 3: ZIGZAG PATH TO GROWTH FOR SPENCER AND BEN

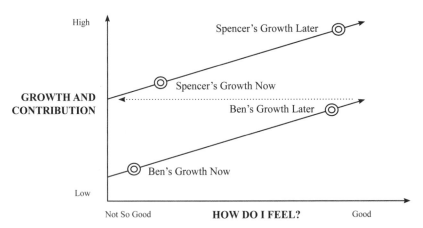

Ben is in the stage in his understanding of his math homework where he doesn't feel good and understands little of the math he is tasked to accomplish. The more he studies, however, the more he'll understand it, and the better he'll feel. Like my bike example, he will move up and to the right of the diagonal line of the zigzag path to growth. When he moves to the top of the diagonal line, all will be well in the Fonbuena household … at least for a while.

Here comes the tricky part of the zigzag path to growth. Just when Ben is beginning to understand the current math problems and feeling good about school and math, he'll be introduced to another new concept that he won't understand, and he won't feel so good in the beginning. And so the process is repeated as he progresses through basic math, to algebra, then eventually on to calculus and beyond. As he moves up the "growth and contribution" continuum, he will zig and zag through the "how do I feel" continuum. Spencer has to go through the same process. Spencer just happens to be further up on the growth and contribution continuum. So Ben and I decided to put down the math for a while, and we just talked about this zigzag path to growth. I told Ben that math will get better, and the difficulty he is experiencing now won't last forever. I assured him that it won't be long before he thinks the problems he struggles with now will be really easy. He took comfort in my reassurance.

However, I also told him that as we progress through math, we are going to go through the process all over again. All of a sudden he looked a bit depressed. I don't blame him. Think back to the monkey brain. In essence, my message to him was, we are going to do everything possible to help him feel better, and then we are going to make a deliberate decision to do something that does not feel good, just when we were feeling comfortable and celebrating our success. If I were him I'd be thinking, "Are you crazy? Why would you do something that doesn't feel good when doing something that feels better is an option? Good question. My answer to this puzzle would be, "feeling good is not our only criteria." Growth, character development, fulfillment, mission, and contribution are also important, and in the long run, such improvements are our goal. He just looked at me as if to say, "Can I talk to Mommy?" I could tell he wasn't convinced. Then I told him that in those tough moments, both Mommy and I would help him. He didn't seem to mind the concept of going through hard moments so long as he wasn't going to go through them alone. He stopped crying, got up off the couch, and with a new resolve started working on the math homework again. Like my son Ben, most of us would be willing to go through tough moments and eventually get to growth and contribution, so long as we know we won't go through them alone. Otherwise our monkey brains wonder whether it's worth the pain, and our lizard brains wonder whether we are going to get eaten in the process.

Let me just insert a couple of side notes here. There are times when we go through growth at a high level as well as at a steep incline, and we enjoy every moment of it. For example, we have a neighbor whose daughter can't wait to get to school every day. She takes the most difficult classes and relishes in the challenge of learning. Then she comes home and can't wait to share what she learned, even to those who aren't interested in listening. She just loves learning. I have a friend who loves to exercise and looks forward to the hard moments of a workout. For these people the growing pains still exist; they have just adjusted to it and have put more emphasis and focus on the growth that will come from their growing pain and less on the growing pain itself. For most of us, however, we do feel the growing pains more acutely, and it takes more of an effort. I wish it were easier, but mostly it's not. Once in a blue moon it is easier, and I'm grateful for these instances. Either way, I know that there is no getting around the growing pain. There is only going through it. The more we realize that it is a normal part of our growth process, the better we handle the growing pain.

I wanted to mention one more thing about the growing pains. I am not referring to a masochistic tendency here in which we enjoy pain for its own sake, and we stay there in the name of growth. No. I'm interested in growth and fulfillment and the joy that comes from it. If some growing pain is required and such pain is normal, then I'm fine with it—only to the extent necessary—but pain for pain's sake is not sustainable or healthy.

Let me give another example of the application of the zigzag path to growth. I was going over this concept with a business executive. From time to time, the productivity of some of their staff was starting to decline. As with many organizations, the growth of their company has some correlation to the collective professional growth of all of their employees. To improve the company, this executive had considered or tried nearly everything imaginable including product creation, strategic partnerships, quality initiatives, additional marketing strategies, compensation structures, and systemic improvements. In other words, he had done everything except asking more of his team. He had asked more "from" them in the past but not more "of" them. In the past he had asked them to "do" more, but he had never challenged them to "be" more. Yet he knew in his heart that what needed changing was in the hearts and minds of his team members (remember the distance between heaven and hell). Some of his staff didn't want to go through the effort of changing and improving. They were getting weary.

He needed his team to be comfortable with growing, even if it meant making mistakes. He explained the zigzag path to growth and committed that he, along with his team, was willing to go through growing pains right along with them. He likewise needed to grow if the company was going to move up from the plateau where they found themselves.

I told that executive about another successful executive who was asked in the prime of the company's success their secret to their company's achievement. His quick reply was "double your failure rate." My executive friend created a culture where growing pain was a necessary, normal, and desirable part of achieving their goals. As a result, not only did they succeed, but they also created a team committed to continuous improvement.

Remember in chapter three, we used the weaving metaphor, where we wanted to develop in the fabric of our lives, the warp of character, and the weft of goals and activities? The growing pain we have been examining in our zigzag path to growth coincides with character development. The more we persist and persevere through the growing pains, the stronger our character becomes as we are stretched.

Character cannot be developed in ease and quiet. Only through experience of trial and suffering can the soul be strengthened, ambition inspired, and success achieved.

—Helen Keller

Look at the individual zigzag path to growth another way as illustrated in Figure 4. With each cycle up the zigzag path to growth, we first go through growing pain. Deep down we know this, and simply acknowledging this reality is half the battle. The other half of the battle of solving this equation is simply going through the growing pains and realizing and remembering that the growing pain won't last forever. It may feel like forever, but there is always an end. There is no going around, but only through. When we persist and endure, at some point we'll move up the growth and fulfillment axis as we gain more expertise, and we'll move further right on the "feel good" axis as our confidence increases.

Figure 4: **ZIGZAG PATH TO GROWTH**

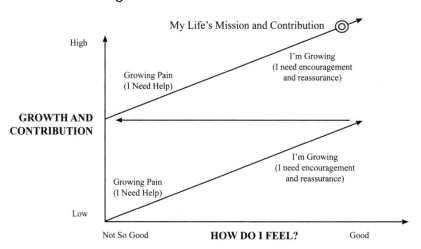

The toughest part is the growing pains area, and this can be made so much easier if there is someone there to help us. We would rather not do this alone. Our monkey brains, which prefer pleasure over pain, will surely continue to remind us to get help or get out. When I mention getting help, it doesn't mean someone will take the growing pain away from us. That would defeat the purpose and only encourage dependence. I'm talking about getting the kind of help beyond our current abilities. For example, my son Ben didn't understand his math homework, and no amount of persistence or positive mental attitude would have made a difference. He needed help, because it was simply beyond his current understanding at that time. Like Ben, most of the time, we don't need a lot of help. We just need a little bit of help at critical times in strategic areas. Think of specific people who have been there for you in your moments of growing pains. They were life savers. Of course the more we realize and appreciate how important assistance from others is in these critical times, the more we'll feel the empathy and need to help others in their "growing pains" moments. We generally appreciate giving and receiving help in equal measure. Once we get past the toughest part of the growing pains, then what we need is encouragement. We long to have and will appreciate the reassurance that we are on the right path, and we need to simply stay the course. We're grateful for those who help us quiet our inner doubts that creep in from time to time in our journey to success. Once you achieve and celebrate your successes, you can only linger for so long before the voice inside of you longing to "be" the person you want to be says, "Let's take another trip up the zigzag path to growth to the next level."

Don't wish things were easier, wish you were better.
—Author Unknown

When I look at the longevity of the Redwood trees and Bristlecone Pines, I am grateful for the lessons they teach. As I have seen people consistently and persistently apply the individual zigzag path to growth, their natures are changed. They see the growing pains as part of the process. They worry less, because they recognize that hard times won't last forever, and in the end they know they will grow and be better. They anticipate the growth opportunities and the accompanying growing pains that will surely come again, and they recognize that with each successive cycle through the zigzag path to growth, their courage, resolve, and character is stretched and strengthened. Their capacities and abilities are magnified. Remember the warp and weft metaphor. At the top of each growth cycle they celebrate the feeling and the knowledge that they are steadily realizing the people they want to be. This is the head and heart being aligned. People do grow and become role models in their chosen pursuits whether they came from ideal conditions like the Redwood trees or harsh conditions like the Bristlecone Pines. Metaphorically speaking, these role models are not as affected by the fires from without and disease from within that seem to plague others around them. They just keep growing no matter what.

HEART TRANSPLANT

By now you recognize that this book is not your typical time-management book. Most time-management books and courses focus on "doing" on the assumption that with greater efficiency the "being" will somehow automatically happen. This book approaches time management from the opposite direction, putting a greater focus on building the foundation of "being." We begin with the heart as well as the mind. The activities we've mentioned are important and make all the difference.

A word of caution is needed now, however. Consider for a moment what happens with those who undergo heart transplants. A diseased heart is removed, and a healthy heart is put in its place from a donor. The body, recognizing the new heart as simply foreign, begins to attack it. If left to take its natural course the body will reject the new heart and the beneficiary of the transplanted heart will die. To combat the natural tendency for the body to reject that which is foreign, medicines are given to the patient. The medicines need to be taken with exactness, and when the body adjusts to the new heart the patient can live for many more years. Interestingly, some patients are casual with taking their medications, because they feel good at the moment. Consequently such a short term view can end up shortening their lives.

When we talk about using our time differently by creating habits of prayer, meditation, and studying scriptures and inspirational literature, it is like getting a heart transplant. It is an equally new experience when we deliberately cycle up the zigzag path to growth. These new habits require a change of heart and not just a change of mind and habit. They require exactness and consistency. We recommended prayer or connection with meaning, both morning and night as well as daily. We also suggested daily study of scriptures or inspirational literature.

In the beginning, if it is not currently a habit, our lizard brains and monkey brains will reject it. After all, they each want to dominate, and much of society's activities are geared toward lizard- or monkey-brain type of activities. Remember that our intent is to use our time in such a way that our divine brains will be the dominant brains. Be exact and consistent. Resist being casual about prayer or meditation. Be diligent in studying scriptures or inspirational literature. Persist until such divine-brain activities are no longer foreign activities, but you see them as an integral part of realizing the person you want to be. Remember that the most important decision you can make is to have your divine brain be your dominant brain. These activities will help to make it so.

One of the great benefits that will come from these activities is to develop your power of discernment. To discern means to sift, to separate, or to distinguish. Prayer or meditation, studying scriptures or inspirational literature increases our ability to sift and separate those things that will help us realize the person we want to ultimately be, versus counterfeits that give only fleeting satisfaction. In our overview of the six allegories, each allegory addressed a question regarding building a culture of being more and not just doing more.

Question from our overview: In the allegory of the tree, why is a focus on character development a necessary part of time management, and what difference does it make?

Answer: Just as the Bristlecone Pine and Redwood trees achieve longevity because they can fight fires from without and disease from within, so can we experience extended success if we can have a barrier against activities and thought patterns that distract us from our path towards being the people we want to be. The development of character creates such a barrier of protection.

To-Be Action Plans from the Allegory of the Trees

- First, commit to making your divine brain your dominant brain.
- Second, begin and end each day with divine-brain activities consisting of prayer or meditation and studying scriptures or inspirational literature.
- Third, continuously move up the zigzag path to growth, understanding that growing pains are just part of the cycle. Persist through the tough times and get encouragement along the way. If encouragement from others is in short supply, be your own cheerleader. In the end you'll grow, feel better, and move towards your mission.
- Fourth, provide help, encouragement, and reassurance to others as they move up in their growth cycle.

Consider these four to-be action plans as part of your time-management philosophy.

CHAPTER EIGHT

ALLEGORY #2: OXEN PULL

FOR thousands of years before the invention of tractors and other farm machinery, oxen have been yoked together and used to pull out tree stumps to clear a field, to plow, and to do other work on farms. The oxen were an integral part of life for many farmers whose livelihood depended on the oxen for the heavy burdens of farming. Today the contribution of the oxen is celebrated with oxen-pull contests in different parts of the world. Two oxen, yoked together are hitched to a sled, and they pull the sled for a designated distance. All of the oxen teams that can pull the sled will move on to the next round. With each round, weight is added to the sled. The team that can pull the most weight wins.

Much like the oxen-pull contest, each of us goes through life with our own unique loads. From time to time, weight is added. Sometimes the load is temporary and other times more permanent. In a time in which we value our independence so much and the idea of self-help has such an allure, sometimes we try to pull our loads all by ourselves. It's more difficult that way. We may even succeed from time to time, but with each successive addition of weight, the difficulty feels more like multiplication. We'll eventually need help. The oxen, when working together, can pull more than the sum of what they can each pull separately. Similarly, we can do more when working with others. Although the allegory of the Bristlecone Pine and Redwood trees reminds us of what we can do individually to be the people we want to be, the allegory of the oxen pull counsels us that there is a limit to what we can do alone. We need other people, and other people need us.

Interestingly, in these oxen-pull contests, the farmers try to find the best combination that would give them the highest probability of winning. The winning combination for the oxen pull involves first, individual strength and training, and second, the team's ability and willingness to work together. It is possible to yoke a trained and an untrained ox together with the hope that in time, the untrained ox will learn from the trained one. This takes time and could work eventually, but you wouldn't want to begin the training process during the contest. The same would hold true when it comes to teamwork. It takes time to create the consistency and coordination to maximize individual strengths in a way that will eventually combine to create great teamwork. In the oxen-pull competition, a smaller pair of oxen, when contributing to each other's strengths and working perfectly in unison, can pull more than larger teams not working in partnership.

Individual Character Strength

Let's take a look at the parallels between the oxen pull and our own lives. First is the importance of individual strength. The reason we mentioned the allegory of the tree using the Redwood tree and the Bristlecone Pine is to highlight the need for individual strength. The greatest reason we want to have sufficient individual strength is to have the confidence and preparation to work with others and create a multiplying effect as an end result. Independence and individual strength is the foundation for teamwork. There's no other way around it. To illustrate, have you ever worked with anyone who seemed to be working with a hidden agenda? That hidden agenda is that person's attempt to compensate for a lack of independent strength of purpose. When teamwork is required, and a member of the team knows deep down that she is not prepared to effectively contribute to the team, she resorts to her hidden agenda to try and compensate for her lack of preparation or lack of strength of character. This applies at home as well as at work. Have you ever seen your kids resort to quarreling when you give them something to work on together? They may resort to the blame game when they don't feel they have the strength of character, purpose, or ability to do their part to finish a task.

Have you ever seen the same thing happen at work or any role for that matter? Disputes happen much more readily when there is lack of individual strength within members of the family or work teams. There is no way to mask it. When family members or work colleagues squabble, the tendency, as the parent or executive, is to try to solve the immediate problem at hand. Do you ever wonder whether you are addressing only the symptom, when the root cause is a deficiency in individual strength, and consequently the cure is to go back to helping build individual strength?

Again, the foundation for building individual strength is to first make up your mind that your divine brain will be your dominant brain. I can't emphasize enough the need to make sure that you daily go through a regimen of divine-brain activities first thing in the morning and the last thing at night. The more you do this as part of your time-management discipline, the more likely you will engage in more divine-brain activities during the rest of the day as well. The other course of action to gain individual strength is to persist moving up the zigzag path to growth.

We Need to Work With Others

Another parallel between the oxen pull and our own lives is the importance of seeing the value of working with others. It is interesting that in most countries a day is designated and celebrated as a day when the country became an autonomous and independent nation. Independence is a great achievement. We also celebrate independence when we graduate, get a driver's license, or open our own new company. Yet, we celebrate less frequently or at least more quietly, the times when we work with others to produce wonderful results. I'm not aware of any national holidays called "Teamwork Day" or "Collaboration Day." Usually, however, most of us spend the majority of our time working and interacting with others. We need to celebrate and hold in higher regard the opportunity and privilege we have to work with others. Just as we set goals to be independent, we also need to set goals to work effectively in teams. Of course, sometimes certain people simply drive us crazy, but seen through a different mind-set and heart-set (remember that heart and mind combination again) we'll have an appreciation for what others can add to our lives and feel reverence for the contribution we can make in the lives of others.

Consider that we live in a time that is more complex and interconnected than the world has ever known. Using the oxen-pull analogy, there is more weight to pull on the sled as a result of the complexities of life in the 21st century than ever before. Independence and individual strength may be a first step, but it is no longer sufficient to meet the demands of a fast-paced and ever-changing world. Independence is only intended to be the first step. It is amazing how corporations all over the world have quickly realized the need to form strategic partnerships and alliances just to maintain a competitive edge. On the personal level, however, most of us are still clinging to the independence we have been taught and celebrated. We need to start thinking in terms of teams, or we could find ourselves inadequately prepared and insufficiently informed even in our personal lives. We could find ourselves exerting so much effort to pull our sleds by ourselves and not see them moving forward. Working with others is not just good idea, but a necessary one.

Charcoal Briquettes

In everyone's life, at some time, our inner fire goes out. It is then burst into flame by an encounter with another human being. We should all be thankful for those people who rekindle the inner spirit.

—Albert Schweitzer

Look at charcoal gathered together in a barbeque as a metaphor for the importance of working with others. When the charcoal briquettes are gathered together they produce more intense heat, and the charcoals are red hot. If you separate one charcoal from the rest, it quickly cools. Of course, you can fan the single charcoal to maintain the heat, but it would take tremendous effort just to come close to the level of heat it had before you separated it from the other charcoal. Now put the same charcoal back in the middle of the coals again, and you will notice it will quickly regain the red-hot glow without much effort. Similarly, we would do better when working with others effectively than trying to do everything alone.

What Is All That Noise?

At the start of the oxen pull, the team will start to pull at the command of the trainer. Consider for a moment, the amount of noise that exists in these oxen-pull events. There is the noise that comes from other teams and trainers. There is the noise the come from the spectators with their ooh's and aah's. There are the noises that come from different distances. The noises themselves are all different. The oxen team, however, cuts through all the noise and listens for the voice of the trainer—no one else. The trainer's voice is near, clear, and familiar. The teams are familiar with the voice of the trainer through consistent training and practice. Just as the oxen team has a trainer, we also need a trainer whose voice will be familiar, clear, and near to us. It is easy to hear the voice of a trainer if everything else is quiet. The question is whether or not we have each paid the price to recognize the voice of that trainer, can hear the voice clearly—even when there are other voices around—and most importantly, whether we will respond appropriately to the trainer's voice. Before we look at choosing a trainer, let's take a look at the other voices that may get us confused.

Other Voices

There are so many voices in the world, each trying to get our attention. Some of those voices shout bad advice, while others grab the attention of our lizard brains or monkey brains. All the while there could be storms brewing in our own lives. The key for us is to determine which voice is worth our heed. Why is it that we can be so easily distracted at times by other voices that would take us off course? It would be helpful to look at the organization of other voices. It takes more than just deciding which voice to listen to; there is also the matter of how often we should listen to them. The voices around us are not just varied, but unrelenting. As we choose to listen to the voice of character, remember to listen to them more often than we listen to other voices. Let's take a look at nature of the voices around us by looking at two voices in particular—television and advertising.

I remember in high school one of my classmates was writing about aliens from a far-away galaxy. These aliens sent spies to the earth to figure out what types of creatures the earthlings were. After careful observation, the alien spies went to their leader and reported that the earthlings were highly religious and devout creatures. The leader wanted to know what lead them to this conclusion. The alien spies reported the following:

- Earthlings lived in homes where there was a room dedicated for their religious worship.
- They worshipped an object that they listened to intently.
- The spies reported that the earthlings worked hard to earn a living and then would buy furniture so they could sit comfortably in their homes and worship this object.
- The earthlings organized their furniture so that everyone could have a good view of this object of worship.

- There were times when friends and other family members would come over just to worship this object together. After friends and family were done worshipping, they would leave.
- The earthlings worshipped this object during mealtimes. When it wasn't mealtime, the earthlings brought in food between meals, so they would not get hungry during their worship of this object.
- The spies also said that some of the earthlings worshipped this object every night.
- The children worshipped after school, on Saturdays, and first thing in the morning.
- The rest of the family would take turns worshipping on the weekend.
- There were even times when just the men worshipped this object, and they seemed to get very excited from time to time during worship.
- Everyone seemed to always be very attentive, and there was little talking.
- Sometimes as the earthlings worshipped this object, they cried together, laughed together, and there were very few things they did more consistently than worship.

As you have figured out by now, the alien spies concluded that the center of worship was the television.

There is nothing inherently wrong with television. TV can contribute good information and entertainment to our lives. This is, however, an example of what can happen, when we don't choose carefully and deliberately the voices we listen to. It is so easy to get distracted with enticing voices that would take us off our course. There are many businesses and organizations that are committed to influencing the thoughts that go into our minds, as well as feelings inside our hearts. These influences will affect our behavior if we're not vigilant. Let's go back to the oxen-pull allegory for a moment. Over time and after a great deal of practice, the oxen team can learn to recognize and follow the trainer's voice above all the other noise. The wrong voice has the same effect. If we listen to the wrong voice over time and with great frequency, we would follow bad advice and move away from progressing toward the people we want to be.

Consider the following question for a moment. How long you can endure before you feel an absolute urge and need to turn on the television, listen to the car radio or your portable music player, surf the Internet, play a computer game, or check the e-mail just one more time, just in case? Most people couldn't make it for a day. If, however, you can resist for an extended period of time, congratulations! Really! You know that pulling off such a feat requires being able to listen to your inner voice long enough that you can block out the other noise. A friend of mine once made an off-the-cuff comment about listening to his music while running a marathon. He said, "I couldn't be alone with just my thoughts for the length of a marathon." It's interesting how we can be so familiar with the noise and other voices around us, yet we can be unfamiliar and maybe even uncomfortable with our own inner voice.

Unrelenting Voices

How do they do it? How has the popular media crept into our lives to the point that we don't even recognize their grasp until we try to break free—and only then do we discover how difficult it is to escape? Advertisers and companies know that marketing and advertising is not an event. It is an extended process. It is nearly impossible to go through a typical day and not get inundated with advertising from the radio, television, Internet, mail, billboards, and the products themselves. The advertising done today is more clever, ubiquitous, and consistent. The intent of all organizations who advertise is to have you use their product or service if you haven't already, or gain your loyalty if you have. It is the life blood of any organization. That is why marketing and advertising are permanent departments and activities in companies. Conduct your own investigation, and the next time you watch a show for a complete hour, figure out how much time is spent on commercials. According to some estimates, in the 1960s there were about nine minutes of commercials for every hour of a programming. Now there could be as much as eighteen minutes of commercials. The length of the commercials has been shortened from about a minute in the 1960s to less than thirty seconds in many cases currently. This means that not only are you spending twice as much time watching commercials per hour, but you are also watching the commercials from as many as four times more companies in a given hour of programming. Advertising is an unrelenting voice.

Not only are companies deliberate and consistent in their marketing strategies, but they are also methodical. When I mention marketing strategy, let me define strategy as resource allocation. This is an important definition that implies that any company when considering its marketing plan must decide, with its limited resources, what it will do and what it won't do. The intent of creating a strategy is to channel limited resources and then focus. They go through a SWOT analysis. SWOT is an acronym for Strengths, Weaknesses, Opportunities, and Threats. This analysis will help narrow down potential options. Careful consideration is given as to product, price, promotion, place, packaging, position, and people. This process further clarifies a company's marketing strategy. The SWOT analysis and 7 P's are common considerations and practices in marketing. My intent here is not to go through a lesson on how to create a marketing plan, but to simply point out that the voices we hear all around us do not happen by chance. Every word used, the tone of the message, the voices we hear, the pictures we see with the varied colors, sizes, and textures go through a sophisticated process that we can only begin to imagine.

I'm not suggesting that we have to go through a complex process to find our own voices. However, I want to point out that we cannot be casual or haphazard in our approach. Businesses and other organizations take their messaging very seriously. If companies were casual about their marketing strategy, it could threaten their very existence. If we are casual about the voices we listen to, we might jeopardize our progress toward being the person we want to be.

CHOOSING YOUR TRAINER

In this allegory of the oxen pull, the importance of the voice of the trainer cannot be overstated. If the winning combination of the oxen pull is individual strength and teamwork, the voice of the trainer affects both. After this big set up, what is the voice of the trainer? Character!

The formation of one's character ought to be everyone's chief aim.
—Johann Wolfgang von Goethe

I believe the reason why character should be everyone's aim is because it helps us to pursue perfection and be the people we want to be. When I say perfection, I'm not referring to being free of faults or weaknesses. Too many of us get caught up in this definition and goal of being free of fault. When looking at the 13th century definition of the adjective perfect, it means complete. The 14th century definition of the verb *perfect* means to bring to full development. When we are choosing to be governed or trained by the voice of character, we are choosing words, natural laws, or principles that help bring our lives to full development.

The application of these words, helps to bring out the very best—the divine—within us. When we weave character development into all of our activities, (remember the warp and weft in our weaving analogy) we are piloting our lives to a culture of being more and not just doing more. Staying with the weaving analogy for a moment, there is a legend and a phrase called the Persian flaw. The legend says that in ancient times, the rug makers in Persia were a deeply-religious people. They believed that only God is perfect. To show their devotion to God, when they made their rugs, they would deliberately include a small faulty stitch, a flaw, into each Persian rug. Similar legends exist in Asia as well as in North and South America. These flaws don't make these rugs less valuable, but more valuable. Though not perfect (without flaw), these rugs are valuable, because they were made with great care and skill. Isn't that what we all want—to live a life with purpose to which we give our very best efforts, even if there is an occasional flaw? Then in the midst of doing the very best we can, our character is strengthened and refined.

Our character is really just another part of who we are, and we need to nurture and develop it as we would our body or mind and every other part of who we are. Choosing to be governed by powerful character words will help us be complete or perfect. These powerful words need to be near, clear, and familiar to us. We need to hear and apply these words with at least the same deliberate consistency as competing voices who shout their bad advice. Let us consider at least one character word that can help us be perfect. That word is: *pre-forgiveness.*

Pre-Forgiveness

The first character development word you need to examine for yourself is the word pre-forgiveness. (The second, third, and other words will be your choice) I have been fortunate enough to have had a boss who has been a tremendous mentor for me—Chuck Farnsworth. I still remember my first day on the job in his department. Like all of the other positions I have ever had, he went through the typical logistics for the first day on the job—what to do, what not to do, benefits, forms to fill out, etcetera. And then he took a few minutes that would change how I would view leadership roles. He told me about his relationship with the rest of the team and what he hoped would be our relationship. He told me I was pre-forgiven. I was puzzled initially and wanted him to expound on what pre-forgiveness meant. He told me he was sure I would make mistakes, because we all make mistakes. He told me to remember that if and when, I make those mistakes, that I was forgiven for them. I remember thinking to myself: *Is this guy for real?* At the time, I didn't know him well. Giving him the benefit of the doubt and wanting and hoping that he was genuine, I wanted to live up my end of the bargain to be pre-forgiven. In exchange for being pre-forgiven he wanted two things. First, he wanted me to tell him of the mistakes. Second, he wanted me to tell him what I learned from my mistakes. He taught me that if all I did was confess, it would not have much value. He said, "Tell me what you learned, so we can all learn. I look at mistakes as investments. I want to see return on investment."

The notion of being pre-forgiving with others is a wonderful and sacred trust. There is a caveat however. This is a two-edged sword. It can quickly build trust when implemented sincerely, but it can also destroy trust and create cynicism quickly if not handled with care. I would recommend not creating the expectation of pre-forgiveness to anyone at first, because before you can truly pre-forgive someone else, you need to pre-forgive yourself!

Before someone makes an offense or a mistake we need to give him the benefit of the doubt and see every person as a person of great worth, talent, and as being capable of contributing in significant and brilliant ways. I define forgiveness as continuing to see someone as a person of great worth, even after an offense. In other words, I can see the divine in others even if their actions are motivated by monkey-brain or lizard-brain thinking. I know they have divine brains, because we all do. Don't get me wrong. I'm not saying forgiveness is the same as trust. Trust is something a person must earn. Unconditionally seeing someone's potential and worth is a mind-set and heart-set. (Remember the distance between heaven and hell—heart vs. head that we mentioned earlier.)

There is a price that you need to pay to be able to pre-forgive someone else and always see the divine in her. The price is to consistently see the divine in you, and recognize it clearly enough to pre-forgive yourself. This is the first voice that we need to pay attention to, and it needs to be clear, near, and familiar. We will invariably all make mistakes, and we can get derailed quickly. Learn to quickly forgive yourself in the midst of occasional mistakes, and continue to see yourself as a person of great worth, potential, and strength. (Remember, strength is one of the components of a strong member in the oxen pull.)

I want to reiterate once again that the first and most important decision we can make is to decide that our divine brains will be our dominant brains. We need to use our time wisely by first making sure that we go through the daily exercise of using our divine brains first thing in the morning and the last thing at night. This is our best line of defense against the lizard-brain and monkey-brain bombardment we will surely have throughout the day. As we make this a habit, our natures will change and we will see the divine in ourselves. Only as we see the divine in ourselves can we pre-forgive ourselves. Pre-forgiveness is simply a reminder that our divine brains are our dominant brains. Only as we pre-forgive ourselves can we pre-forgive others.

The best place to start a culture of pre-forgiveness is with you. Follow the process that my boss Chuck shared with me. First, confess to yourself, or in other words, have the awareness that you made a mistake. Second, take the time to really think through your mistakes and ask, "What have I learned from this?" Remember, you can choose to make your divine brain your dominant brain, and pre-forgiveness is a divine brain thought. You can do it. Your own perfection or completeness and full development is at stake. Persist, even when you make mistakes on occasion. We all have to practice being our own best cheerleader. Learn from the past mistakes, and don't dwell there. Keep moving forward.

Ponder for a moment what your family or workplace would be like if everyone were pre-forgiving. What would you anticipate would be different in a family or work environment that was pre-forgiving compared to one that was not? Jot down a few ideas.

_____

_____

_____

Go the other way. What if your family or work culture were not only void of pre-forgiveness, but people felt pre-punished? Life is tough enough as it is without feeling that you have to defend yourself from people who are supposed to be your allies. What would your family or workplace be like if people felt pre-punished or pre-judged?

_____

_____

_____

Remember, time is opportunity measured in units of possibilities. When you create a culture or shared value of being pre-forgiven, beginning with yourself, you are facilitating perfection or bringing yourself and others towards full development.

You, yourself, as much as anybody in the entire universe, deserve your love and affection.

—Buddha

ASSEMBLE YOUR ADVISORY BOARD

Where do we start when it comes to working with others? We have been taught all our lives to be team players, but rarely have we been told to put together a team. It is interesting and wonderful to know people with talents different than my own. I'm at awe when I consider how each person is not only unique, but uniquely divine. Most of the time we are just resigned to think: *I wish I were more like that person.* Well, we're not and will never be like any other person, because we are all unique. However, our lives can be enriched just the same by the gifts, experience, and advice of others.

How? Assemble your own advisory board! Be deliberate. This doesn't require you to hire anyone or file legal documents. You are not forming an organization, but you are forming an advisory board to help you run one of your most important organizations—you! For some this will be a new concept. Regardless, most of you will recognize that you have already put together an impromptu team. You may just call them a select group of friends or family members. What I'm suggesting requires you to be more deliberate and exact.

Let's take a look at a typical advisory board member and the legal language that is used to describe that person.

- Board members must act honestly and *bona fide* (in good faith).
- A board member shall perform his or her duties in a manner he or she reasonably believes to be in the best interests of the corporation.
- Performs duties with such care as an ordinarily prudent person in a like position with respect to similar corporation would use under similar circumstances.

Can you think of people right away in your circle of family, friends, and acquaintances, from whom you would appreciate getting advice, because they would act "in good faith," have "your best interest," and perform their duty with "care" and "prudence"? You may consider adding board members who would:

- Help with your growth and development
- Listen
- Review your performance and be a trusted accountability advisers
- Give input and advice
- Give support and evaluate your progress
- Validate, affirm, and help you tap into your potential
- Bring expertise that would be helpful to you
- Provide guidance and direction

These people can be living or deceased. They may come from any part of your life. How many board members should you have? How often should you meet? Should the meetings be informal or formal? Do you meet all together or meet with each separately? What should be discussed? You are the chairman of the board. You decide. You may want to add to or change your board as your circumstances change. In the oxen-pull allegory, we mentioned that the winning combination is first, individual strength and training, and secondly, the team's ability and willingness to work together. Working together means your advisory board responds to the same trainer's voice. This is the most important criteria in your selection process. We mentioned the importance of the voice being the voice of strong character. As you consider those you would include in your advisory board, select people with strong character, whose moral purpose is the same as yours. Choose people who use their divine brains to dominate their thinking. They may have different opinions and abilities, but choose members whose character will strengthen your own. Tap into the power of teams. You have been part of a team of one sort or another your whole life. It is now time to switch your thinking from being a team player to be the one to assemble a team.

BEING YOKED TOGETHER

Assembling your personal board of directors is a powerful idea that will give you greater wisdom, clearer direction, and assurance. However, your advisory board is only that: a team you have assembled to give you advice in helping *you*. The execution of your great ideas, however, is another matter. Use your advisory board to get input for all of the roles you have in life.

Continuing on with the analogy of the oxen pull, as you consider how you will accomplish your goals, you may need to work with other teams. In your family life, it would be members of your family. In your professional life, it would be your colleagues. At church, they are the members of your congregation. In your child's sports team, it may be the other parents. Being yoked together with others is a forceful and dynamic idea. Just as the oxen need time to learn to work together, so we need to be deliberate and take the time to learn to work with each other as a team. Being yoked together is not delegation, distribution of labor or even giving inspiration on the sidelines. Being yoked together is working alongside each other, united in effort and not just purpose. Being yoked together means going through the process establishing character traits, principles, or values you want to share. This is a process you will need to discover together. As the mom, dad, or executive we need to do activities *with* them just as much as they need to do it *with* us. Let's take a look at a work and family examples to illustrate.

Yoked Together at Work

As a sales trainer, participants in my class truly appreciated what they had learned, but many of them wanted to see the training practiced in the "real world" and not just in the sterile environment of the classroom. Granted, some wanted to transfer their learning to the field because it was their learning style, while others didn't quite believe that the theory in the classroom would work with clients. Others still didn't want me to work with them in the field, because they felt comfortable learning it on their own and would rather stay in a classroom environment. Regardless of their learning style, personality, or circumstance, I had the opportunity to go in the field to sell *with* them. In every case, their learning improved dramatically, our relationship was strengthened, and their results improved.

I worked with a senior sales manager who enjoyed working directly with clients alongside his sales managers and many of the sales people throughout each year. When he spoke, everyone listened, because they knew Steve knew what he was talking about from the point of view of the rank and file sales person. When Steve challenged them to do hard things, they believed him, and if they didn't believe him, it wasn't a big concern. Each sales person knew at some point Steve would help them believe, because he was going to sell *with* them and grow in their experience together. When other more senior members of the executive team would speak, it was sometimes met with skepticism, not because it didn't make logical sense. The sales team questioned the credibility of some of the senior executives because they'd never sold *with* those executives before. The sales team would question whether the executives' ideas were crafted in a board room without any connection with clients. The other reaction to the executives' counsel was to give a polite gesture, take a mental note, and ask Steve about it later.

Yoked Together at Home

The same principle applies at home. Have you ever told your children to go out and play? What they really need is for you to go out and play *with* them. Perhaps sending our children to some sort of camp or putting them on a club teams is a good idea, but regardless of your skills, playing *with* them is what children value. Many mothers, including my own mother and wife, have been great examples to me. My wife, for instance, not only plays with our children, but she is there consistently, spending time in the important daily crossroads in our children's lives. She is there every day to wish them a wonderful day first thing in the morning. She is there to read a story in the evening before bedtime. She has done this so consistently that even our twenty-one-year-old appreciates and participates still in the bedtime stories to our younger children when she is home from college during semester breaks. My wife is there to help clean their rooms *with* them. The children are there doing yard work together with Mom (and sometimes Dad). She invites our children to help cook the meals *with* her. You may think that working with them may defeat the purpose of teaching them to work independently. Our experience is different. It is more than *knowing what to do*. They must have *wonderful feelings and memories* associated with the simple things such as cleaning their rooms, helping cook meals, and doing yard work. Such is the power of working *with* them. The consistency pays great dividends. My children feel comfortable coming to me when the challenges are small. Perhaps they need help with a particular math problem. However, when the issues are jugular, my children approach Mom first. Why? Because she has paid the price for years and she has been there for them daily. The bonds of love and trust are created day after day, in the seemingly small daily events. When hard moments come, or metaphorically speaking, when it's time for the oxen-pull contest, our children knew where to go first. My wife and children are yoked together. If time is spent together in the common and regular events of life, great bonds are created to last a lifetime. Allow me to share a story from my wife to illustrate.

Mom and Quilts

Mom seemed to have a sense of urgency to get Margaret's quilt finished. It was still months until the wedding, but she was happy to have all the help she could get with the quilt. More quickly than I thought possible, the quilt was finished, bound, and tucked away as the focus turned to sewing dresses for the grandkids and bridesmaids. I loved having her at my house as we puzzled over what size of dress to make for who, how to adjust this pattern or that one, cutting, sewing, picking out seams, ironing, and admiring the work in progress. As I saw Mom move a little slower and sleep in a little later, I was almost shocked to think that maybe she was actually getting older. She could always run circles around all of her six daughters and one son.

Some of my earliest recollections from my childhood were of playing under a quilt set up on frames, which for us, made a great fort or play house. We played while listening to the visiting of the grownups. Sometimes it was at our house, other times at one of my Grandmas' homes. In fact, quite often, my grandmas would be found quilting on each other's quilts. We lived next door to Dad's parents and Mom and her mother-in-law were the best of friends. As we played under the quilts, only occasionally were we scolded, when we bumped the frames, nearly knocking the quilt over. I am sure that more than once we were the cause of pricked and sore fingers.

As I grew up, my desires to join the circle of quilters grew, and Mom always found a place where I could help until my stitches became a bit more acceptable. I never could equal Mom's stitches, even though I got pretty good. People would see her hand quilting and think it must have been done on the sewing machine. But she never felt she was too good to let anyone try their hand at quilting. She was always willing to pull up another chair and let someone new join the conversation and love that was shared as the quilting was done. In fact, she was very proud of the big stitches that were sewn into quilts by her grandchildren. She was so pleased that they wanted to join the fun and learn the art she loved so much

As both of my grandmothers passed away, Mom took on the tradition and task of making a quilt for the wedding of each grandchild, which she continued to do for many years. Mom not only quilted, but if she heard of someone needing a quilt right away, she would piece one together and tie it. I remember one summer day we tied four or five quilts for her niece whose children were in need of some blankets. What fun it was as we worked together, laughing and talking as we tied the day away.

She spent a week one summer with two of my girls, teaching them how to piece a quilt and then coming to our home to help us quilt them. She quilted baby quilts for babies who didn't have a grandma to quilt one for them. She would quilt alone if there was no one to help, and although I never found anyone who could equal her stitches, she always preferred to have as many as possible sitting around the quilt with her.

Little did we know as we quilted on Margaret's quilt (who was the last of her six daughters) that she would barely live to see her married. She was diagnosed with cancer Easter weekend and passed away six weeks later on Mother's Day, a couple of weeks after the wedding. As I wandered around my childhood home after the funeral, I was surprised to see that she did not have many quilts around the house. Even her favorites which had taken months to piece together and many more hundreds of hours to quilt, had been lovingly given away. I began to realize as people shared their condolences that there were hundreds who had been the recipient of Mom's love of quilting, either through having the privilege of spending time sitting around her frames and quilting with her, or by being wrapped in her warmth and love of the actual quilt. I was lucky enough to have been blest by both.

✳✳✳

The common activity of not just quilting, but quilting together, the mother *with* her daughters and loved ones, was the difference. This is a great example of the allegory of the oxen pull. The mother, daughter and grandmothers may have been generations apart, but their strength of character and relationship was equal. Like the oxen, they heard the voice of the trainer— love. Over the years the voice of love was clear, near, and oh so familiar. They were yoked and tied together through quilts, for life, and beyond.

TEAMWORK DEFINED

Remember that in the oxen-pull contest, the winning combination is individual strength and teamwork. I would define the very best of teamwork as two or more people who each have gained great individual strength by the consistent and dominant use of their divine brains. Each team member is deliberate in the development of his or her own character. The members of the team may have different backgrounds, personalities, talents, and skills, but what binds them together is their commitment to being familiar with and having confidence in the same trainer's voice of character and moral strength.

This voice is clear, near, and familiar. Teamwork is channeling this trainer's voice towards a common cause and contribution to others. The very best teams—whether the teams are families, work teams or any other group—are pre-forgiving of themselves and others. Instead of judging and simply stating the faults of another, they see the faults of others as the monkey-brain and lizard-brain thinking creeping in, and they wisely put all their efforts into helping their teammates get back to divine-brain thinking. They help their family and teammates tune in to the trainer's voice of character, and their teammates help them do the same when needed. The very best teams are full of hope and nurture the divine in others. This is the lesson of the oxen pull.

The allegory of the oxen pull is about seeing the value and importance of other people in our lives. As we'll discover in the allegory of the three-combination lock, there is a sequence and a methodology to maximizing what we can learn from others.

> **Question from our overview:** In the allegory of the oxen pull, who are the people essential to helping us be the people we want to be, and how will we identify them?
>
> **Answer:** Just as an oxen team working in unison can pull more weight than the sum of what they can pull separately, so we can pull life's load more easily when we work with others.

To-Be Action Plans from the Allegory of the Oxen Pull

- First, be a strong team member by having your divine brain be your dominant brain.
- Second, assemble your own advisory board with people of strong moral purpose or character—or in other words, people who use their divine brains as their dominant brains.
- Third, assemble other teams in your other roles and work *with* them with the intent to weave character development with goal achievement.
- Fourth, reduce or eliminate the unrelenting voices and noise such as the programs on television, Internet, lizard-brain and monkey-brain dominant thinking people, etcetera that distract you from hearing the voice of the best that is in you.

CHAPTER NINE

ALLEGORY #3: THREE COMBINATION LOCK

AS we each examine our lives, we are really trying to lead three lives simultaneously—our lives in our communities, our family lives, and our personal lives. The community life is the one that all our neighbors, work colleagues, and even strangers see us living. It is the life where others can see what we do, hear what we say, and sense us thinking and feeling. For most of us, this is the life where we spend the majority of our time. This is the life where we don't just transact, but in the midst of our interactions, we create opinions of each other. This is where we make value and character judgments of each other. This is where someone might say we are kind, result-oriented, talented, outgoing, gracious, thoughtful, and so forth.

It's easy to see why so many of us spend so much time in our community lives and enjoy it. When I mention community life, this would include our roles at work, church, civic duties, volunteer organizations, and so forth. It is full of associations with many people. Perhaps there is even recognition, and maybe there are awards involved, or perhaps there is monetary compensation. This is the life where we get a sense of belonging and importance. This is where our monkey brains get really excited. Certainly having other people singing your praises is very gratifying. Below is a visual representation of time spent mostly in community life in relation to perhaps family life and personal, unseen life. If we spend too much time in our community life we may feel disconnected with those in our family life, and our family will feel disconnected with us.

Figure 5: OUR THREE LIVES

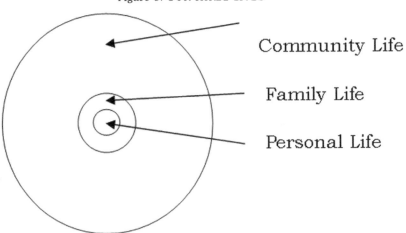

We also have our private lives, which only those few who are closest to us know about. This consists of our family members or a very select group of friends. These are the people we feel most comfortable with, and those with whom we feel we can afford to let our guard down, if you will. These are the people with whom we can share what we really think and feel, and we know they will have the discretion, care, and the wisdom to handle such information. A disconnect between people can occur when each person has a different focus. For example, my wife, Julie, is a stay-at-home mom, and the focus of her time is spent handling everything at home as well as teaching and raising our children. She is preparing them for an uncertain future, and I am amazed at how she does what she does. Being a mom is the hardest job there is. I truly believe in the notion, "Dad might work from sunrise to sunset, but Mother's work is never done." Obviously, while my focus might be greater outside the home, or in the community at large, my wife's focus is in the home. To keep our relationship strong we need to make sure that we put enough focus on each other and not drift apart.

You may experience a third scenario in which a member of your family is consumed with only himself or herself. You may have heard the expression, "I may not be much, but I'm all I think about." Each person at some point, is self-absorbed, trying to answer the question, "Who am I, and where do I fit in?" Figure 6 is a visual representation of three people who focus their time in different areas.

Figure 6

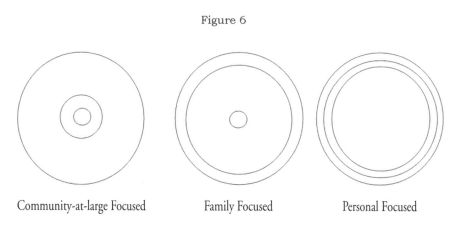

Community-at-large Focused   Family Focused   Personal Focused

Having members of our family or private lives with a different focus is normal. We are all in different stages with different concerns. The problem is when these differences cause us to drift apart. For those of you who have been married for a while, do you ever wonder whether your spouse is becoming more and more of a stranger to you over time? I hope not, but if we're not careful it can happen. Do you sometimes look at your children, especially in their teenager years, and wonder whether their minds have been abducted by aliens? Your teenager may be changing so much and so fast that it's hard to keep up. How do you get such unique personalities, each with a separate focus, in the same household on the same page? We'll get to that!

The third life is the unseen personal life. This is the life that only *we, personally* know about, until such a time that we are comfortable enough sharing with those in our private lives. Within our unseen personal lives are our innermost hopes, dreams, struggles, and fears. This is the life where we may feel the strongest and most vulnerable at the same time. This is the life in which we try to reconcile in our hearts, minds, and souls the meaning and value to our existence, in the context of our family and community life as well. This unseen personal life is our core. We know we need to give ample focus to it, while at the same time we may feel guilty and selfish for doing so, because there is so much that needs to be done in our other lives.

These are three interconnected lives indeed, and the importance of each of our three lives will vary, depending on what is going on in that particular season of life. As I look back in my children's lives, early in the elementary school years, they each seemed to balance personal life, family life, friends, school, sports, music, and everything else with relative ease. Sure, there were traumatic episodes, crying, new discoveries, deep friendships, big fights, but all of these events seemed to happen within the context of the same day; they bounced back quickly, forgave easily, and had short memories. After dinner and a decent night's sleep, they were ready to tackle the big bad world all over again the following day. A teenager's life revolves around self as they are maturing and becoming more independent. Though clumsy at times, they are trying to figure out life as best as they can. With most adults, I find that reconciling these three lives is more difficult with each passing generation. It seems that the older we get, juggling these three lives become increasingly perplexing and complicated.

How do you manage time in the context of these three lives while those around you are all trying to do the same? Let me suggest three approaches to improvement, from the most common to the most effective.

THREE APPROACHES TO IMPROVEMENT FIRST: OUTSIDE-IN APPROACH TO IMPROVEMENT

This is the most common way that each of us hopes change and improvement will occur. The *outside-in* approach basically means that we hope circumstances and people will change to suit our needs. It requires the least amount of work and is the least demanding on us personally. Examples could include wishing the economy would change to suit us better. Perhaps we wish our customers were more cooperative and that our colleagues were easier to work with. Perhaps we would wish our spouse or children would exercise greater wisdom and judgment, without any effort on our part. This is the wishful thinking approach to change. Of course, every once in a while things just work out for us—the traffic light turns green when we want. The grocery line we are in is actually quicker. We might have an unexpected wonderful turn of events, or every now and then, our children clean their rooms without being asked, coerced, or threatened. Ultimately what we want is an approach that would give us the highest probably of succeeding. This approach has the lowest probability, and we know it, but we have to try it or at least wish for it just the same.

So we try another outside-in approach. This approach would be making a variety of changes without necessarily changing or even examining ourselves. For example, in the home, we might try to implement a series of rules. It may even work for a time, but eventually it gives way to other restraining forces, such as our children figuring out how to get around the rules. We then come up with more rules, and we realize that after a while we have so many rules we can't even remember all of them. We can even have so many rules, that they begin to contradict each other. Sometimes the rules turn punitive and demoralizing. From the sociologist Emile Durkheim:

> When mores are sufficient laws are unnecessary. When mores are insufficient, laws are unenforceable.

Whether the context is home, work, or the attitudes and social conduct of nations, more rules and laws usually result in little more than simply having more rules and laws.

In the workplace we may introduce new mission statements, new strategies, or install high-tech systems. We can try reorganization, implement new compensation systems, and like the home, it works for a while, but we soon discover that it can only be sustained at a high cost.

The following appears in Robert Townsend's book *Up the Organization*:

> I was to learn later in life that we tend to meet any new situation by reorganizing; and a wonderful method it can be for creating the illusion of progress while producing confusion, inefficiency, and demoralization.

If reorganization doesn't work, changing management is usually the next order of business, along with sending people to leadership training. When reorganization and management changes don't work, usually enough time has elapsed between changing the structure and changing management that a new book comes out on reorganization under a different name, and we start the cycle again. After a while, another book comes out on leadership, under a different name, and training continues with a round of leadership musical chairs. The appeal of the *outside-in* approach is the hope of improvement with the least amount of effort. Juggling your three lives with this outside-in approach is hoping that those in your private or family life and public life or life in the community at large will change or improve on their own, so that you don't have to.

SECOND: INSIDE-OUT APPROACH TO IMPROVEMENT

Most people would agree that in the long run an *inside-out* approach is more effective and more predictable than the outside-in approach. The inside-out approach basically means that we need to work on ourselves first. We redefine our challenges from "how circumstances and people should be different (outside-in)" to "how can I be different" (inside-out) to get a different result. When we focus on changing ourselves, we then put less focus on being a victim. We also put greater emphasis where we have the greatest influence—ourselves. When we change, we define the circumstances around us differently. For example, with an outside-in approach we may see the world through the lenses of challenges and problems. Through the inside-out approach, however, we could look at the exact same circumstance and see opportunity and a chance to make a contribution. As different industries and even nations go through varied economic cycles, you have heard countless stories of those who have made their fortunes in the midst of economic downturns. Those who take an outside-in approach are paralyzed, staring at the problem, while those who take an inside-out approach make their fortunes—and both are looking at the same data.

> A pessimist sees the difficulty in every opportunity; an optimist sees the opportunity in every difficulty.
>
> —Winston Churchill

In the home, one may see a recurring and annoying problem, while someone else may see no problem at all. For example, one particular summer day I came home from work, and I couldn't get into my garage. Between the street and the garage in my driveway were my children's bicycles, toys, sidewalk chalk, and so forth. I parked in the street and told my children to remove the clutter from the driveway, which they happily did, and I then parked in the garage. The following day (I think you can see where this is going), I saw the same jumble once more. Again I told them to remove the clutter (using a little more stern voice), and they obeyed just as they had on the previous day. On the third day, to my amazement, I saw the same clutter for the third day in a row.

If I took a strictly outside-in approach, I could define this driveway problem a number of ways. First, I could identify the kids as being the problem. I could rationalize to myself that for one reason or another they just don't understand what I'm trying to teach them. Second, I could identify the problem as the bicycles and toys. I could say to myself, "I knew we shouldn't have bought so many toys and bicycles. They have too much stuff." Third, (in a moment of temporary insanity) I could identify the problem as my wife. I could storm into the house and demand to know, "Honey, what have you been doing all day?" By the way, this is the kind of mistake that can only be made once!

Looking at it from an inside-out approach, however, my wife reminded me that the children had been happily playing in the driveway every afternoon. There wasn't a problem until I got home! When my wife and I discussed it, neither she nor the kids considered it a problem. As far as my concerns, the simple solution was for me to call home before I left the office, and the kids would clean up the clutter before I arrived. I went from taking an outside-in approach in which I saw a problem, to a very simple inside-out approach in which my concern was resolved in one conversation.

A challenge with the inside-out approach, however, is that even though we may cognitively agree it is a better approach, sometimes we're not quite sure how to implement it. Based on the Winston Churchill quote about an optimist focusing on the opportunity instead of the difficulty—if we do see things in a pessimistic way, are we suppose to just flip a switch, and all of a sudden we're optimists? We're not quite sure where to begin or what to do next.

Another challenge with the inside-out approach is, not knowing what to change about ourselves, not knowing how much change is enough, and whether we are going at it the right way. How do we get to the point where we look at the world through an inside-out approach, (understanding that we need to look in our own mirrors for the answer) without feeling like whatever we do is not good enough or there is always something wrong with us?

THIRD: LEARN FROM WITHOUT; THEN GROW FROM WITHIN

This third approach is most effective and has elements of the first two approaches. There is a voice within each of us that can sense the answers existing outside ourselves. We know we don't have all the answers, but we also understand that answers do exist out there somewhere, and we need to access answers in so many areas. And so we look for answers outside ourselves—outside-in. We go too far, however, when we expect these answers to come wholly from the outside in, simply for the asking—like a genie in a lamp who can grant to us any three wishes. From time to time, we may receive answers in full, but more often, we merely get clues and guidance. This is a good thing. Whatever you want to call it, there is a force in the universe that won't give us answers for the asking, but instead gives as hints. There is the danger of dependence—and laziness if we're given the answers too easily. Consider this story from the October 1950 Reader's Digest.

> In our friendly neighbor city of St. Augustine great flocks of sea gulls are starving amid plenty. Fishing is still good, but the gulls don't know how to fish. For generations they have depended on the shrimp fleet to toss them scraps from the nets. Now the fleet has moved ....
>
> The shrimpers had created a Welfare State for the ... sea gulls. The big birds never bothered to learn how to fish for themselves, and they never taught their children to fish. Instead they led their little ones to the shrimp nets.
>
> Now the sea gulls, the fine free birds that almost symbolize liberty itself, are starving to death because they gave in to the "something for nothing" lure! They sacrificed their independence for a handout.

I think people can become like that too. It would be nice if the answers to life's questions were just given to us like scraps or handouts from the universe. However, it would create a dependence and slothfulness that would be just as dangerous to us as it was for these sea gulls in this story. The seriousness of such dependence is multiplied when you consider the ever-changing nature of our world today. We can't afford to be less, as life today demands more. We don't want just the scraps from the universe anyway. Rather, we want all the universe has to offer. That would require effort on our part. We are trying to prepare ourselves and our children for an uncertain and unpredictable future. The Reader's Digest story continues.

Let's not be gullible gulls. We ... must preserve our talents of self-sufficiency, our genius for creating things for ourselves, our true love of independence.

The fact that effort is required to achieve what we want, is both the challenge and the blessing. Recall the zigzag path to growth in the allegory of the tree. We go through growing pains on our way to personal growth and fulfillment. The key to learning from without is to identify and understand the hints from the universe, and determine what to do with those hints.

This third most effective way of changing—"learning from without then grow from within"—has two parts. Learning from without is about learning natural laws through the living examples of other people. Growing from within is having enough conviction and desire to take what we have learned from others, and emulate those lessons in our own lives.

LEARNING FROM WITHOUT

When we look at learning from without, we want to take note of three hints.

1) Results
2) Natural laws or character traits that apply
3) The people who adhere to them

The essence of learning from without is to understand there are natural laws that govern all results over time. I like the concept of *law*, because it implies something that is fixed, predictable, and orderly. These laws, however, are not made by man, nor are they enforced by man. They operate regardless of our awareness, acceptance, or support. They just are. Just as there are laws—such as *gravity*—that govern in the physical dimension, there are natural laws that govern all results. The results may vary in the short run, but in the long-term the results are predictable. It may be helpful to use other words, such as *formulas, principles, rules, recipes, order,* and *blueprints* to clarify the nature of these natural laws. There's an element of certainty and rigidity to them. In the long run, it's cause and effect, though deceivingly fluid in the short run. Other synonyms that would help us understand these natural laws are *traits, virtue, character, disposition*, and *quality*. Again they are not just nice trite words. They are the roots that produce the results we want. Just as the Bristlecone Pine and Redwood trees both need nutrients even though their circumstances are vastly different, we need the nutrients that natural laws give us to produce results. Although we'll go into more detail on how to take full advantage of these natural laws in the next chapter, some examples of these natural laws are *vision, empathy, love, contribution,* and *integrity.* These words are not an exhaustive list by any means, and you may choose these and/or other natural laws to govern your life.

The last part of learning from without is seeing the power and efficacy of these natural laws in the lives of those around us. In short, we need heroes, mentors, and models who live by these natural laws. Models are valuable to us because of our three-part brains. Making a conscious decision to live by these natural laws is divine-brain type of thinking. Our monkey brains, however, are not quite sure what to make of these natural laws—not sure whether it's going to feel good or not so good. When we are not sure whether something will feel good or not, our monkey brains or that part of us that says social intelligence is important asks, "Who else is doing it, so that we can find out whether they felt good about it or not, and then we'll decide?" Without models, we hesitate to venture out on our own. Remember, we mentioned how the monkey brain can hold the divine brain hostage. Having a model allows our monkey brains to tell our divine brains, "It's going to be okay. I feel better about it now that someone else feels good about it, and I respect his or her opinion. Let's go for it."

In the history of mankind, there are those who have gone before us having struggled through similar experiences that we are going through now, though they may not be exactly the same. They have lived their lives based on these natural laws we have mentioned. Without people as examples, words such as *vision* and *integrity* are merely words. They are just abstract ideas. However, when we see these words acted out by those we trust, admire, or rub shoulders with daily, these words become real and powerful to us. Without such examples, we can look at these natural laws and readily dismiss them. We can get so caught up in the uniqueness of our situations that we miss the whole point. We can rationalize ourselves right out of the answers we seek. Our monkey brains can tell our divine brains, "I may not know everything, but I don't feel good about this," and then we move on to something else. Learning from without is both understanding with the mind and feeling with the heart as we see those we trust live by such natural laws.

Living your life according to natural laws such as vision, empathy, love, contribution, and integrity takes a certain amount of faith, because even though they may produce the results we want over time, that may not be the case in the short run. However, expecting high achievement over time without these natural laws is a much more difficult proposition. Imagine trying to be the person you want to be and increasing your achievements by being visionless instead of having a clear vision, being cruel instead of empathic, being filled with hatred instead of love, living a life of selfishness instead of contribution, and dealing in corruption instead of integrity. In the long run, having your divine brain as your dominant brain is better than having your lizard brain and monkey brain dominate your life.

When my father was thirty-three years old, he was a high-ranking officer in the Philippine Army. He took great pride in his profession, and he excelled in it. Thinking more about our family than his career, he resigned from the military, and at great expense, we immigrated to the United States. He had to start his career all over again in a completely new industry, not to mention a new country. My parents with their four children lived with our uncle and their family in their small apartment in Los Angeles. I still remember one of his first jobs was at a furniture manufacturing plant. Even as a young boy, I was puzzled as to how he could go from commanding armies—a bright future at the station in life that he had envisioned—to leaving it all behind and taking a lower-paying job that was well below his ability level. I asked him about it as a young man, and I can still see the smile on his face. He said, "Oh that. If my goal had been just for me, we would have stayed. We didn't come here for me. We came here for you." That was my first recollection of really understanding the words *vision, sacrifice, love*. At that moment I wanted to become the kind of man that he is, and I wanted to become the kind of father he is to me. Words such as *vision, sacrifice*, and *love* came alive to me as I saw them personified in my mother and father.

Each of you, more than likely, had a person or persons come into your life as a living example of certain character traits. Maybe that person was a parent, grandparent, teacher, neighbor, or friend. Because character is such an integral part of this time-management philosophy, write down the names of three people you admire and who personify character traits that you want to emulate in your own life.

Name _____

Character traits they lived by

_____

_____

_____

Name _____

Character traits they lived by

_____

_____

_____

Name _____

Character traits they lived by

_____

_____

_____

I hope you can gain a greater appreciation for those who have been the role models for you. Thank them for the courage they had to live their lives according to natural laws or character traits. Consequently, I hope you can be more judicious about the people you select to be part of your personal advisory board. They can liberate you and your divine brain from the bondage that our monkey and lizard brains can put all of us in. Not only can your advisory board lift you, but those individuals can also help give you ideas that you have not considered. We all should recognize the impact these role models have on us as well as the impact we have on those who look to us to be their role models.

Grow from Within

Your vision will become clear only when you can look into your own heart. Who looks outside, dreams, who looks inside awakes.

—Carl Jung

Once we have learned from without, we then have an example, a pattern as to how to grow from within. Those who have lived their lives by adhering to natural laws and have been the type of people we would like to be, serve as examples to us, and their lives become blueprints for us. These wonderful people become our heroes, models, mentors, and we desire to emulate their character traits into our own lives. Through the lives of these models, we can see, in great detail, their triumphs, the corresponding obstacles, and how to rise above challenges that we wouldn't otherwise anticipate. We pay close attention to what they do, say, think, and even feel. We pay attention to how they prepare to achieve their successes. These people may not be absolutely perfect (none of us are), and so we need multiple models. Each of us is unique, so again we need multiple models customized to our unique personalities and circumstances. We look for the very best, the divine, in our heroes and models.

In our private or unseen lives, we begin to live our lives in like manner as our models. We begin to form habits and live our lives according to natural laws. Like planting a seed, in time, our habits of *vision, empathy, love, contribution*, and *integrity* blossom and bear fruit. Not only do they bear fruit, but they do so time and time again. The more we see desirable results, the more our confidence grows. Our confidence in such living grows in our hearts as well as in our minds. These habits that we form are not just stuff we put on a list and check off as we do them, but rather, these natural laws change our very nature.

Once we can sense that our very nature is changing, it is so exciting. We get so excited by the positive results from living according to strong character traits that we want to share it with those in our family and others in our private lives. In time we so greatly appreciate the transformation and improvement in our own lives that we want to help our loved ones do the same. We in turn become a model for others. If our lives have truly been lifted, we want to lift the lives of others. "Truly" is the operative word here. This means we are convinced of the power and efficacy of natural laws in our hearts and in our minds. We have implemented these natural laws or character traits and know firsthand the results that can come from adhering to them. We must keep working on implementing these natural laws or character traits until they become so obvious to us that we surrender our wills to those natural laws or character traits.

Learning from without and growing from within, takes effort, but it is well worth the effort. I hope your results and your excitement make you not only want to share with your families, but that you would also want to share with those in your community life—your neighborhoods, work colleagues, and even strangers, for that matter. Share your experience and insights of how adherence to natural laws or character traits has helped you.

This approach of learning from without and growing from within naturally resonates with most people, because we have all experienced it to some degree. Look at it this way. Can you think of a person who saw you in a more favorable light than you saw yourself? Because such a person has come along, you have "learned from without." Because someone has become the source of light or inspiration for you, haven't you in turn desired to become the source of inspiration for someone else somehow, which caused you to grow even more? That's one example of learning from without and growing from within.

Allow me to give another example. Just before my wife and I were married, we were busily trying to find an apartment where we would live. When we found an apartment, we wanted to furnish it with a few things, but like many newlyweds, we were broke. The only furniture we had was a lamp. That was it. Picture a one-bedroom apartment with just a lamp. Even though the apartment was small, it was so empty that it would echo every time someone spoke.

My wife's friend from work, Carolyn, knew of our circumstance and wanted to speak to me in private. A few days after our conversation she had fully furnished our apartment. In the kitchen/dining area she got a microwave and a microwave stand. She also managed to find a dining room table with four chairs. In the living room she got an area rug, a sofa, a loveseat, a couple of plants, a chair, and some decorations for the wall. Of course, we contributed our lamp. In the bedroom she furnished a new bed, dressers, and two night stands. All of these furnishings are not something she could readily afford, but she wanted so much to do this wonderful thing for us. When we were all in the apartment for the first time, marveling at our fully-furnished apartment, Carolyn said that they were in a very similar circumstance when they were married. Someone had also furnished their apartment and simply asked in return that when the opportunity arose in the future that Carolyn and her husband would do the same thing for another couple. She thanked us for helping her fulfill her promise, and asked us to do the same for someone else in the future. This was such a profound experience for my wife and me, and we look forward to fulfilling our promise to Carolyn. Learn from without then grow from within.

> What man actually needs is not a tensionless state, but rather the striving and struggling for some goal worthy of him. What he needs is not the discharge of tension at any cost, but the call of a potential meaning waiting to be fulfilled by him.
>
> —Victor Frankl

Most of us can recall times in our lives when we grew exponentially, and there were tough moments associated with that growth. Many times people tell me they want to get back to when they grew so much and lived a life of constantly learning from without or learning from others and growing from within. It's almost as if there were different seasons of life in which we experienced such growth. When I have asked these same people why such growth didn't continue, given that it was so beneficial, the most common answer is, "Life just got so busy!" Well, life probably won't be less busy any time soon for most of us. If in the midst of such busyness we could get back to living such a life, with a time-management tool that would integrate natural laws or the strengthening of our character, we would indeed become the people we want to be.

Ultimately what people want is to have a rich personal life, rich family life, as well as a life of contribution to the broader human family, whether it's through professional work or volunteer endeavors. In the context of our three lives, we want to unlock and unleash the potential we all feel is inside of us. Look at it as a three-combination lock that you probably used in high school. Do you remember the directions to open your combination lock? You had to turn the dial clockwise to a specific number lined up to a notch and then turn to the left for the second number until you passed the second number for the second time around. You then turned clockwise again to the third number, and when you pulled on the shackle the lock would open. What would happen to me, however, was that every now and then, in my rush, I would only turn counterclockwise to the second number once instead of twice, before turning clockwise to the third number. When I pulled the shackle, it wouldn't open. There was no other way to get the combination lock to work other than to start over and try again. There were no shortcuts on the combination lock. It is much the same way with our three intercon-nected lives. If we want to unlock and unleash the full potential that is in each of us like the unlocking of a combination lock, there is a process that works—and there are no shortcuts. Learn from without, then grow from within.

The lesson from the allegory of the Bristlecone Pine and Redwood trees is how to continuously grow while at the same time fight our fires from without and avoid disease from within. Although there is much we can do individually to grow, the allegory of the oxen pull reminds us how we also need others who wish to obey the same natural laws as we pull life's load. The lesson of the allegory of the three-combination lock is to have the context of the three lives we lead and the need to learn from without and then take the lessons learned from other people and grow from within. We need to take a look at the next allegory of the four seasons to take a deeper look at how exactly we learn from without. What follows the allegory of the four seasons—the allegory of the five golden rings—will allow us to take a deeper look at how exactly we grow from within.

> **Question from our overview:** In the allegory of the three-combination lock, what are our most important roles, and how can we improve in each of them?
>
> **Answer:** We lead three interrelated lives.

1) Our personal lives
2) Our family lives or private lives
3) Our community at large or public lives, which include our work, church, civic, and other roles.

- Like unlocking a combination lock, to unleash our potential there is a sequence. Learn from without and grow from within. This means we have the blessing of learning from those we admire in our family life and public life by looking at the character traits or natural laws that made them effective in their lives. Their examples become the pattern for us to follow to grow from within.

To-Be Action Plans from the Allegory of the Three-Combination Lock

- Remember your three interconnected lives,

  1) Your life in the community at large,
  2) Your family life, and
  3) Your personal life.

  Make sure ample attention is given to all three.

- Learn from without, Learn from the lives of other people by observing how they have applied character traits in their lives. Identify people whose character traits you would want to emulate in your own life.

- Grow from within. Now that you have examples of people who live according to specific character traits, commit to live your life and use your time to weave the warp of character of weft of activities and goals.

CHAPTER TEN

ALLEGORY #4: FOUR SEASONS

IMAGINE the four seasons: winter, spring, summer, and autumn. They happen in a predictable sequence, and each season plays an important part in the ecosystem. Plants, animals, and people alike respond to the rhythm of the seasons. Each season gives its distinctive beauty and feeling as well as bringing balance to the ecology.

This allegory is connected to how we achieve results consistently. Achieving results also has seasons, sequences, and patterns. As we have just examined in the allegory of the three-combination lock, we mentioned the importance of learning from without and growing from within. In this allegory we are going to take a more in-depth look at how to learn from without. We will not only look at how results are achieved, but how character is connected to results.

One of the four seasons represents our achievements. How do we realize achievements, and is there a predictable pattern to achieving them? Consider this question. Would you agree with me if I said that that your achievements stem from the things that you do and/or say? In the many times I have posed this question the answer has always been *yes*. It is self-evident. What we do and say has a great impact on what we achieve. Results or achievements represent one season. The things we do and say that lead to our achievements represents a second season.

ACHIEVEMENT

DO/SAY

To illustrate, consider for example an athlete who practices his sport for hours each day. When the practices (do/say) have been repeatedly well-executed, the athlete or team is likely to do well (achievements). Think of the example of a manager who pushes a new strategy with every opportunity he can find (do/say), and consequently turns the team around (achievements). Study the salesperson who makes a high volume of prospective client calls daily, no matter what (do/say), and consistently hits her goal (achievements). Ponder about the parent who deliberately and consistently spends time with his children, whether it's playing, listening, working, laughing, helping with homework (do/say), and has a good relationship (achievements). It's easy to see how consistency in actions and in words, contribute to your achievements.

If people knew how hard I worked to get my mastery, it wouldn't seem so wonderful at all.

—Michelangelo

In the last chapter you wrote down the names of three people you admire and who personify character traits you want to emulate in your own life. To further examine and validate the notion that achievements come from what you do and say, consider these admirable people and ask the following questions.

- What extraordinary results did they achieve?
- What particular actions did they take that led directly to their remarkable achievements?
- What were they consistently doing and/or saying that helped produce better results, where others who may have the same ability weren't as consistent?

The deeper you dig into the success you see in others, the more you will realize that, like Michelangelo, there is a predictable pattern of effort and hard work that leads to achieving results. The more you peer into the lives of those you admire, the more you will realize that in many respects, they are just normal people like you and me, complete with weaknesses as well as strengths. They did and continue to do what most of us have the potential to do, but these role models were just more deliberate and consistent. I've always had the notion that I can do what moms can do. Okay, stop laughing. The difference is, I can only do what moms can do for less than an hour at a time, while my wife, mother, and mother-in-law do their magnificent labors 24/7. The dads like me, who have been left to tend to the kids on occasion, may have had an added appreciation for all that moms accomplish every day. I remember hearing a boy about eight years old reciting a poem when I was only about twelve years of age. I never wrote it down, but I never forgot it.

Mothers are sweet.
Motherhood is really neat.
But all in all, I'm so glad
When I grow up I'll be a Dad.

Mothers do amazing things because of their diligence, vigilance, and consistency. Watching ordinary people do extraordinary things by being consistent is such a hopeful proposition. If they can do it, I can as well. The question is figuring out how these wonderful people are so consistent where others stall. We'll get to that.

Again, one of the seasons in this allegory represents our achievements. A second season is what we do and or say. Yet another season is what we think and feel. Would you also agree with me if I said that what we do and say is influenced by what we are thinking and feeling at that given moment? Like the previous question, when I ask this of different groups of people, time and time again, the answer is a resounding *yes*. It would be the same for us, our role models, or anyone, for that matter. It would also be the same regardless of whether we were looking at great achievements or bad results.

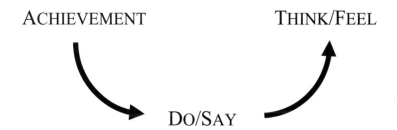

ACHIEVEMENT   THINK/FEEL

DO/SAY

Many people striving to achieve different results have an unrelenting focus on taking different actions. This makes sense, but it's incomplete. You have probably heard the expression that the definition of insanity is doing the same things and expecting different results. It's natural to think that doing things differently would produce different results. This at least works on paper. Yet when it comes to the execution of those actions, many times it is either lacking or unsustainable. When I say lacking, I mean a lot of commitments and promises are made, but there is not much action and follow through. When I say unsustainable, I am referring to commitments we make such as New Year's resolutions. We get off to a good start on January 1st, but our new desired behaviors and changes as well as our resolve are all gone by February 1st. As a parent, have you ever told your children what to *do* over and over again, and yet the changes you wanted don't happen? You may have even posed the question, "How many times do I have to tell you to …?"

Have you ever had team members at work come to you, wanting to know what they should *do*? Have you noticed that sometimes, after you give them your sage advice, they then proceed to tell why your advice simply won't work? Why does that happen? It happens because we may come to an agreement on what to *do,* but we are not in alignment on the *thinking* on such actions or the how we *feel* about taking those actions. For example, we may all agree that exercise and eating a healthy diet is a good thing to *do*, but when it comes time to actually *do* what we know we should, we can *think* of reasons why not to exercise or eat right on a given day, or we just may not *feel* like doing them today.

He who cannot change the very fabric of his thought will never be able to change reality, and will never, therefore, make any progress.

—Anwar el-Sadat

Once again think back to your role models whom you admire, and evaluate how they were able to think/feel differently than most, and how it allowed them to take different actions that most wouldn't take. Ask them how they were able to make the shift in their thinking and emotions. This is a great exercise, because it will give you great insight on what motivates you and what motivates others.

In high school I graduated in the top five of my graduating class. In college I got my first "D" grade in my first year of college when I had never even gotten a "C" grade in any class ever. On the other hand, by the time I got to my third and fourth year of college I got an "A-" in one class, and the rest of my grades were "A+." What was the difference? In my first year of college I was lost. The classes were so different. The huge university was a self-contained city, and it was a bit intimidating to me. For me college was terrifying , exciting, challenging, and fun all at the same time. I hadn't made up my mind and heart, as far as what I wanted from college. I just went with the intent to do my best with no purpose or passion. By the time I was in my third and fourth year of college, my purpose was clear, and I did a much better job with knowing when to say *yes* and when to say *no* to various activities (remember the lesson of selective neglect from the all-you-can-eat buffet). I formed better habits, and I wasn't just trying to pass classes to meet the requirements. I was trying to master subjects that I knew I would be using and would be held accountable for in the workplace. I wasn't just trying to get a degree, but I was also preparing for a career to support a family.

I have seen other students take a different route, where their grades suffered in high school, yet when they got to college, they did extremely well. These students were bright and more than capable but saw no purpose in their education while in high school. When they got to college the light bulb turned on in their hearts and minds, and they really applied themselves. In either case, the difference in what was done and said was highly influenced by the strength of thought and feeling.

In the allegory of the three-combination lock we mentioned the need to learn from without. We are now taking a much closer examination of what precisely to learn from without or what to learn from others as we rediscover how achievements are realized. Again, results and achievements come from what we do/say. What we do/say can only be sustained when the actions and words that will produce the results we want, are in alignment with what we *really think* and *really feel*. In the simple examples on exercise and eating right, the model is self-evident. In the more jugular issues in our lives the model is just as valid and applicable, but it requires a bit more soul searching. For example, what do you really think and feel about yourself? What do you really think about the important people in your life? Are some of those important relationships strained? How do you really feel about those people?

What do you really think and feel about your outlook on the future and the unique contributions you can make? In your quiet and private moments you need to reconcile what you sincerely think and feel. No one except for you can answer this do/say think/feel alignment question in the tough issues for you. This takes humility and honesty and some time to ponder. Remember the distance between heaven and hell. When you reconcile your real intent, your true feelings, and most honest opinions, it is a great victory indeed. Going through this exercise of accurately assessing your thoughts and feelings will give you clarity.

Let's have a quick review. The results and achievements we get stem from the things we do and/or say. What we do and say is influenced by what we think and feel. This begs the question, "If what we do and say is influenced by what we think and feel, what then molds what we think and feel?" In short, it's the voice that we listen to. Remember the allegory of the oxen pull and the trainer's voice? Ultimately then, the voice that we listen to directly impacts our achievements.

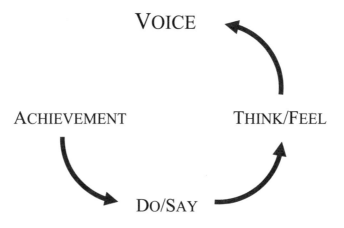

Now let's take a closer look at the voice you may listen to that affects your thoughts and feelings. In essence there are two sets of voices that clamor for your attention. There is your inner voice, and then there are the external voices. There are many external voices that demand your attention. There are the voices from society as a whole, the media, friends, family, work, and other relationships. Each of these voices has an impact on you, however large or small. Some of these voices stimulate your lizard brain and monkey brain, while others are just noise without much value.

The same can be said for your *inner voice*. You have the internal voices that speak nothing more that lizard-brain and monkey-brain type stuff while other voices are just noise. The most important voice of all, however, is your own inner voice of character.

Each person has the inner voice of character that helps us realize our very best selves. Your character resides in the divine part of your brain. Listen to and be true to your inner voice of character. Your own inner voice of character should be the voice that lets you know what value and attention you should give to the other internal and external voices.

> **The only tyrant I accept in this world is the still voice within.**
> —Mahatma Gandhi

I recall the consistent comments I've received from thousands of educators whose experience in the education profession ranges from a few years to decades. When I consult with these educators regarding their students who struggle academically and/or have greater-than-normal discipline problems, I ask the educators what they think is the biggest contributor to the students' challenges. Remember, these are young children from five to about twelve years of age. Without exception, educators observe that those who struggle are the students who listen too much to the external voices of negative influence of their neighborhoods— television, peer pressure, video games—and not enough of their own inner voices of character. Those who struggle later in their teenage years have a different set of problems than elementary students, but the root cause is the same: they listen too much to external voices and either don't know or don't pay attention to their own inner voices of character. To complicate matters, many times these young people also don't have enough caring parental involvement (positive external voices), or they have no parental involvement at all. For those who do have caring parents, too often those parents do not spend enough time helping their children to learn to listen to their inner voice of character. Other times parents are not quite sure how to teach their children to listen to their inner voices. If these children do not learn to listen to their inner voice of character, then their problems will persist and many times worsen as they get older, because negative external voices dominate their thinking and mute their internal voice of character.

I am not suggesting that all external voices are bad, and that we are to be quarantined from the rest of society as a protective measure. I've often thought, "Wait a minute. What about the notion that no man is an island, and it takes a whole village to raise a child?" Unfortunately, relying on the community to help us, or our children, or others to be the best we can be, is no longer as reliable as it used to be. The key is to make sure your inner voice and the external voices that surround you are leading you in the same direction. You need to be selective as to which voices to listen to. Again, not all external voices are bad. Some of these voices include mentors, heroes, people who have lived inspirational lives as documented in history and scripture, and we may even know some remarkable people personally.

What you need to consider as part of your time-management strategy is how to reduce or eliminate the time you spend listening to voices that do not lead you towards your best self. Do not spend time with people or situations that are at odds with your inner voice. Spend more time with people and in places that are uplifting and can validate your inner voice.

With the intent to give balance to our examination, think of your most recent achievements. Just as some of our actions have come from a lapse in character, your proudest actions have come from strength of character. Let's highlight a few of these character traits. Write down one of your specific achievements that has made you feel proud.

_____

_____

_____

As you think about this achievement, would it be fair to say that your actions that led to your achievement magnified your character trait of *integrity* to do what was right and necessary? Wouldn't you say that your proudest actions demanded your character of *courage* to act? More than likely it also took your character of personal *humility* to adjust and to make changes as they were needed? If your proudest actions involved other people, would it be fair to say that you also tapped into your character of *service, contribution* and *love*? I think we don't celebrate enough the strength of character that we exhibit every day or point out and congratulate the same strength of character in others. There is a lot of good that happens every day, and we would all get more of it if we acknowledged and celebrated those instances more often. What would happen if part of your time-management strategy involved paying attention to the character traits you see exhibited every day in yourself and others? The voice that you listen to has a great impact on what you think and feel, do, and say. Ultimately that voice affects your results—whether for good or for ill. As we examine all of the external and internal voices we are exposed to, we can either go in the right direction or not.

> The right direction is the one that leads you towards realizing your best self.
> The wrong direction is the one that does *not* lead you towards realizing your best self.

How do you avoid the wrong direction? When it comes to avoiding the wrong direction, there are so many unique and varied external voices that can take you in the wrong direction, that it is impossible to list them all and simply avoid them. What wrong voices all have in common however, is that they do not lead you to where you can realize your divine and best self. Listen instead to the voice that leads you to your best self. The definition of the right and wrong direction that you see above is a simple divine-brain definition, but it can be clouded easily with lizard-brain and monkey-brain rationalization. Remember *rationalize* means "rational lies." Keep the definition of the right direction versus the wrong direction simple. If you are finding that it's more difficult to count on the community as a whole to help you be your best self, the most reliable solution is to help yourself and also to help those you care about learn how to listen to their inner voices of character. So how do you help yourself or others listen to that inner voice? The first big question you need to answer to more consistently listen to your voice of character is to decide:

What do you really ultimately want?

Deep down, when all the pretense and complexity is stripped away, what you truly want or desire will come down to one of two things—to do what is right or to do what is wrong. Answering this first question will determine your direction. Again, let me define doing what is right as doing whatever is necessary to realize your best self or your divine self and build on your character. Think back to very early in the book when we defined our time-management challenge as weaving together the warp of character and the weft of activities and goals. What do you really want to weave together? When you are engaging in activities that will help you realize you best self, you are focused on the divine brain. When you are focused on divine-brain activities, you are doing the right thing.

Doing the wrong thing, again, is defined as *not* doing what is necessary to realize your best self. When you are engaging in activities that don't help you realize your best self, chances are you are in the monkey-brain or lizard-brain mode.

Having a heartfelt commitment and desire to do the right thing is the first and biggest personal victory you can achieve. Your thoughts and feelings that would yield results are first influenced by your desire to do the right thing or the wrong thing. If you desire to do the right thing or be your best and divine self, this will lead you to the source of best self, your character. Granted, we won't be perfect in always doing what is right versus what is wrong, but the question here is not to analyze your actions but to simply declare your desire. If you are unsure as to whether your desires will lead you toward your best self, consult members of your advisory board and those whose character traits you admire, and get their advice.

In our quest to be our best selves, I believe every person who has had the desire to do the right thing has had set backs at one time or another, and it is certainly human to make mistakes. The second step then after having a desire to do the right thing is to have the desire to pre-forgive. Remember to pre-forgive yourself, and make the commitment to simply get back on course every time you get off course. The older I get, the more I realize the need to make corrections in my life sooner rather than later. Delaying course correction only delays your arrival to being the divine person you have in you. Desiring to be your best self by doing what is right is something we simply need to hold with childlike faith. Little children are quick to forgive and pre-forgive. We need to recapture this mindset.

We mentioned earlier that our thoughts and feelings are influenced by the collective internal voices that we listen to. Looking at the graph below, and on a scale of -100 to +100, with negative numbers representing the wrong direction that leads you away from being your best self, and positive numbers representing the right direction that leads you toward your best self, assess the strength and direction of the internal and external voice that you listen to now. Have your advisory board also assess how you are doing. Compare the two to validate where you are currently.

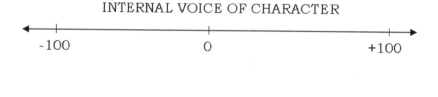

INTERNAL VOICE OF CHARACTER

-100   0   +100

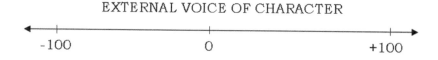

EXTERNAL VOICE OF CHARACTER

-100   0   +100

The strength of the voices you listen to is determined by simply combining the strength and direction of the internal and external voices.

STRENGTH and DIRECTION of VOICE = INTERNAL VOICE + EXTERNAL VOICE

The voices that lead you to your best self, represented by the positive numbers, are your divine-brain voices. The voices that lead you away from your best self, represented by negative numbers, are lizard-brain and monkey-brain voices. As you make commitments to listen to the voice of character, choose which character traits you will emulate in your own life. I hope you took some time to ponder and identify at least three from the exercise on page 104. If not, please take the time to go through that exercise at some point, as choosing character traits to start with is a big part of this time management philosophy that involves piloting your life to a culture of being more, and not just doing more. Consider again the influence that the inner voice of character has on your thoughts, feelings, and eventually on your achievements. Ponder this great quote from Henry David Thoreau.

How can we expect a harvest of thought who have not had a seed-time of character?

—Henry David Thoreau

This is a very interesting quote from Henry David Thoreau, because to me it says we either currently possess strong character (where our thoughts and feelings come from) or we can make a conscious decision to nurture our character now. As we develop our character now, we can harvest the fruits of character later. The development of our character will lead to the maturation of our thoughts and feelings. The evolution and maturation of your thoughts and feelings will improve your behaviors and guide you to know the words to speak, which will in turn improve your results and contribute to your achievements.

Good character is more to be praised than outstanding talent. Most talents are to some extent a gift. Good character, by contrast, is not given to us. We have to build it piece by piece—by thought, choice, courage and determination.

— John Luther

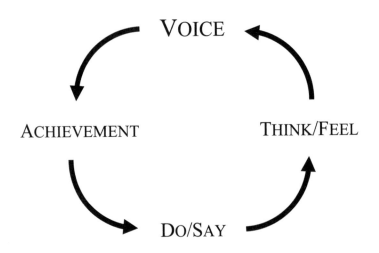

Day by day we can make deliberate choices that will improve our character. We are talking about more than to-do lists. You can call these your "to-be" lists. To illustrate the importance of making small, deliberate decisions, think about your favorite painting. Every painting is a collection of brush strokes. When you are close enough to the painting to examine each particular brush stroke, none of these brush strokes is particularly impressive or interesting. Stand a little further back, and you will see a combination of strokes with different colors—probably going in different directions—and they may seem completely random. It is not until you stand back far enough to see the entire canvas and get the appropriate context that you will see a beautiful painting. Similarly, when we evaluate the character of those we admire, we will see that they do good things consistently, or that they develop their character deliberately, one brush stroke at a time. Like looking at a painting too closely, small and deliberate acts to improve character may not seem like much. Collectively, these seemingly small acts, as you persist, can make of your life a work of art. Don't think, however, that building our character "piece by piece," as John Luther put it, can be delayed until tomorrow. These seemingly small acts can lead to great results, and over a life time transform lives that inspire us all. What would happen if we included as part of our time-management philosophy and practice, the small things that if done consistently over time would build our character?

No man can climb out beyond the limitations of his own character."
—John Morley

No matter how full a reservoir of maxims one may possess, and no matter how good one's sentiments may be, if one has not taken advantage of every concrete opportunity to act, one's character may remain entirely unaffected for the better.
—William James

Some may consider the development of character as separate from the development of the mind or body or relationships. We disagree. Indeed they can be, and most of us have done exactly that. Therein is the missed opportunity. For example, some may have excelled and focused primarily on their work lives (mind) in isolation and at the expense of the closeness to those in their family lives (relationships). Others may have spent so much time and singular focus taking care of their own health at the expense of important relationships. Yet others may spend time developing relationships but not much else. Staying with the four-seasons analogy, having a singular and unbalanced focus on one dimension of our lives would be analogous to having a long drought season year after year. In time, that would create great imbalance and destruction within the ecosystem. I find that most people, however, have already done the hard work of spending time developing each dimension at different times, but the magic is seeing the interconnectedness of each of these dimensions in our lives and developing each dimension appropriately. Understanding how each of the different dimensions work sequentially like the four seasons is the key.

In fact, this cycle that we are referring to as the allegory of the four seasons is something that you have already done many times over. Have you ever been given directions to a place you have never been to before? You are in your car driving, and you know that you are headed in the right direction, but then there's a point when you are not quite sure whether you may have missed a turn somewhere. You then rely on a bit of logic and your sense of direction, and then you arrive at your destination, having taken the shortest path to get there. Of course, you didn't know it at the time you were driving, but looking back you amaze yourself. Developing our character is much the same way.

Every significant achievement you have ever had required that you use strength of character. Earlier you looked back to particular achievements you have had. Examine a few more of your achievements. Do the exercise again or look at the achievements of your family members and other important relationships. Would you agree that to achieve anything, you exercised at least three character traits: first, the courage to act; second, the humility to adjust or change course when needed; and third, the integrity to do what is right and necessary? If your achievement involved others, the fourth character trait you strengthened is the desire to contribute, serve, lift, or love another person.

Consider the relationship between character and results. You can look at it from a formulaic point of view.

$$\text{ACHIEVEMENTS} = \text{FUNCTION of} \left(\frac{\text{VOICE OF CHARACTER}}{\text{DIFFICULTY OF THE CHALLENGE}} \right)$$

Your achievements are a function of the strength of your character (voice of character) in relation to the difficulty of your challenge. The greater the achievement that you want to realize, the greater strength it demands from your voice of character. The greater the difficulty of the challenge, the stronger your character needs to be, to achieve what you desire.

Your voice of character is linked to *integrity*. It is interesting that the root word for *integrity* is *to integrate*, or in other words *to join, orchestrate, or unify*. Integrity is also related to the word *integer*, or *being whole*. The development of the character or spirit is intended to be unified and orchestrated with the development of the mind (what we think), the heart or relationships (what we feel), as well as the body (what we do and say). When it is all said and done, the development of the character is everything. From your character flow your thoughts and feelings. From your thoughts and feelings come your words and actions, and from your words and actions your achievements and contributions are derived. Your achievements and contributions will reinforce your faith and confidence in the continued development of your character. The more you deliberately follow this cycle, the more you will recognize its power and simplicity. In time it will create its own perpetual motion and will lift your life in an upward spiral.

It is a liberating thought that the management of our time is simply and profoundly, the management of our character. The management of our character involves integrating everything we are already doing and making adjustment where we have misalignments.

ACHIEVEMENT CYCLE

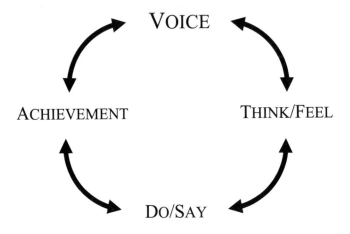

I refer to this cycle as the Achievement Cycle. Initially we looked at this model in a counter-clockwise direction to explain the way it works. Go through your own counter-clockwise examination of your life and get a good sense of your current reality. Then take a clockwise assessment and implement the model, making the appropriate additions, deletions, and modifications to be the person you want to be.

As you look at the four seasons and the Achievement Cycle, making changes begins with listening to the voice of character, which to me, is synonymous with the winter season. Winter is a period of reflection and a new beginning. The winter solstice marks the victory of light over darkness. Winter begins the new cycle of light, life, and growth, and so it is with listening to the voice of character. A focus on the development of your character represents a victory and greater dominance of your divine brain over your lizard brain and monkey brain. Listening to the voice of character enlightens our hearts and minds. It marks a new beginning of growth in the Achievement Cycle. Listening to the voice of character gives greater life to our divine brains.

As spring follows winter, so do our thoughts and feelings spring from our character. Spring represents a time of blossoming. Spring is a time when the weather becomes more temperate. Spring is a period of optimism, of a rebirth, and renewal. Similarly, as you are going in the clockwise direction in the Achievement Cycle and focusing on listening to your inner voice of character, your thoughts and feelings will blossom and become more refined, hopeful, and peaceful. Your thoughts will become more temperate. There will still be ups and downs, but you will discover that emotionally you will become more even and more temperate. Your view of life will be more optimistic as you see the best in yourself and others. You will have a rebirth and a renewal in your faith in all people. Of course, not everything will change immediately, but you will see more of the potential in yourself and others.

Next comes the summer. The summer days are also the longest days of the year in which daylight predominates. Summer days are the warmest days of the year. With the longest days come the shortest nights. Summers are filled with activity and celebration. Summer is a time of festivals, holidays, gatherings, and vacations. Summers give the feeling that time is suspended, and everything seems possible. The parallel for summer in the Achievement Cycle is what we do and say. When your actions and words are deliberate expressions of your character, then your actions and words are filled with that divine light that is within you. Like the summer season, your divine light dominates, and you act with faith and confidence. When your actions flow from your character, everything seems possible, and your actions are inspired and seem effortless.

The last of our four seasons is autumn. Autumn is the season of harvest. As you progress clockwise in the Achievement Cycle, you will harvest greater achievements, and your inner voice of character will seem even more familiar, nearer, and clearer. With each successive cycle, your confidence in yourself, your character, and this model will grow. With each cycle you will strengthen a culture and a mindset on how to be more and not just do more.

Let's do a quick review in our time-management journey from the allegory of the combination lock, to the allegory of the four seasons.

- In the spirit of learning from without and then growing from within, make a list of people you admire.
- From among the people you admire, choose role models that exemplify the character traits you would want to emulate in your own life.
- Go through the Achievement Cycle and learn how your chosen role models and mentors realized their potential.

> ❯ Examine their lives by looking at the voice of character they chose to live by, followed by how your role models think and feel differently as a result of using these character traits as their moral codes.
> ❯ Examine the behaviors that come from their thoughts and feelings. Also look at the words they say. How are their words and actions different, compared to those who achieved less?
> ❯ Look at the results they have achieved as a result of their behaviors and words.

Go through this process a number of times with different people. Choose people you know personally, and even take a look at great people in history and see whether the model holds up. Ask your role models and mentors about their role models and mentors, and see how much merit the Achievement Cycle has for those people as well. Go through the Achievement Cycle a number of times, clockwise and counterclockwise.

If you want to diagnose how results, good or bad, came to fruition, begin by identifying the results. Let's start with good results. Begin by examining the proudest accomplishments of your life. Beginning with your results, go counterclockwise in the Achievement Cycle and identify the actions you took and the words you spoke that directly led to your amazing accomplishments. Now we want to isolate your particular behaviors and words. Continuing in the counterclockwise direction, identify thoughts and feelings that motivated you to act and speak as you did. Finally, pinpoint the character trait(s) you had to draw from as well as the deep desires that you had in your heart of hearts to accomplish what you did. I hope you would take the time and opportunity to celebrate not just your achievements but your strength of character necessary to achieve your remarkable results. Can you see how all the components of the Achievement Cycle manifest in your successes?

It's important to go through the same examination with bad results as well as the very best results. Seeing the contrast will help you recognize where your breakdowns occur and give you clues on how to correct them. The more familiar you are with the model, the quicker you can anticipate where the corrections are most needed in your life. If examining your bad results feels too painful or you think those experiences are too close for you to objectively examine them, turn on the news on TV or the Internet. There's usually a story or two about someone who has been very successful and has recently fallen from grace, causing us to view them much differently than we did before. Go through the Achievement Cycle to see if you can match the rise and fall of these people with this model. You may get new insights. Whether you examine good results or bad, this Achievement Cycle will usually go back to the strength of character or lack of it. I say *usually*, because like the weather, we can have natural disasters in our lives that cannot be foreseen, or we may have wonderful weather that we didn't anticipate. So, you may see an exception here or there. In the long run, however, our results will tend to follow this model. Earlier we defined time as opportunities measured in units of possibilities. Taking the time to go through this model will reveal to you where some of your greatest opportunities lie. Now that we have "learned from without" from your role models as well as your own experience, take what you have learned and grow from within.

Now that you have gone through this cycle by looking at your successes, ask yourself what else you want to accomplish. Beginning with your goals and strength of character, go in the clockwise direction. Consider both the goals you want to attain and the strength of your character from which you will need to draw. What thoughts, processes, and strategies might you need in order to make the achievements you wish for, a reality? Identify and draw from the character traits you already know you possess.

Once you understand the Achievement Cycle, you can see more clearly how you can diagnose your past successes as well as failures through the same model. You can put this model to use in carrying out your future triumphs. Think about your superhero role as a mother, father, or any other role where you are a steward of other people, and how you can use this Achievement Cycle to help you.

Children/Student Example

I was working with a high school where many of the students struggled academically, violence was high in the neighborhood, and community expectations of the children were low. The administration applied strong pressure to bring test scores and grades up. Many of the teachers were still hopeful and optimistic, working hard and doing their best under the circumstances, but overall morale was sagging. All the while, the state's economy was in decline to the extent that negotiations were being conducted involving teacher layoffs, teacher pay cuts, or a combination of both.

In the midst of all of this, some of the teachers took a completely different approach on improvement. Instead of focusing on grades and test scores (achievements) first, they started with character development. They started with telling their students (using my words) that they each had a divine brain. They told their students in the midst of societal pressures, that they had the choice to make their divine brains be their dominant brains, even though all around them were monkey-brain and lizard-brain type of thinking and behaviors. The students, wanting to test the sincerity of their teachers, deliberately made poor choices as it relates to their school work. They wanted to know whether the teachers would use lizard-brain or monkey-brain tactics at the first sign of trouble. You can imagine that the administrators were nervous when they saw that the teachers' strategy was immediately yielding worse results. These select teachers, however, truly believed in the divine potential of their students. These teachers focused on the students' potential and ability to "be," and on their capacity to achieve infinitely more, if the students could discover that the choice was truly their own. The teachers persisted. The teachers saw the divine in themselves and in their students. When the students realized that these select teachers were sincere, the students then acknowledged that the results they were getting were really not what they wanted. That's when everything changed. Although they were behind and had some catching up to do, these students made up their (divine) minds that they were going to rise above their current circumstances and move towards the view that these select teachers had of them. Because of their own determination and new vision, they worked hard and significantly improved their grades. They went from failing to doing well enough in high school to get into college, and eventually they finished college. They often come back to this high school to thank their teachers for believing in them long enough, for the students to believe in themselves. The students were grateful, not just for what they discovered they could do but for realizing what they could be. The students discovered they are people of great worth and potential, and that they have gifts and talents that can contribute greatly to others around them.

The results the administrators had hoped for were achieved, not by focusing on results, but by focusing on the students' voice of character, that if followed clockwise on this Achievement Cycle, would eventually yield prolonged great achievements. Once we go through the metaphorical four seasons of *voice/character, thinking/feeling, doing/saying, and achieving results* in natural order, we'll gain a greater appreciation for the power, beauty, rhythm, and predictability of this model.

Work Example

As far as a work example for the Achievement Cycle, conduct your own informal survey. Ask people you know who they admire the most as an executive and why. Even though you'll be asking people from differing companies and industries, I would venture to guess that the two most common reasons executives are admired have to do with results produced and character. There are those who can deliver results without character, because they have more than enough smarts or they came up with products or services that were are great demand. They don't tend to last long, however. Long-term success requires more than ability and smarts, but in the spirit of the allegory of the oxen pull, executives need the support and effort of everyone in the organization. Everyone in every organization has their lizard brains that ask whether they feel safe with their executive at the helm. If so, they give their jobs their all. Or, do they feel (in the spirit of the insecure lizard brain) that their executive might eat them? If an employee feels unsafe, then it makes sense that she feels a need to allocate a portion of her time protecting her job and herself somehow instead of being wholeheartedly focused on the mission of the company.

Please allow me to offer a word of caution on the Achievement Cycle. There are two reasons I can think of why this is not applied more often. One reason is lack of awareness. This is easy to resolve. Just by having the awareness outlined, you can make great progress. The other part of awareness is having the strategy to execute this model, which will be covered in the sixth allegory. This is divine-brain type thinking and feeling. This is choosing to be divinative. The second reason why someone may not follow this pattern is because the lizard-brain or monkey-brain mentality takes over, and this model is then abandoned. Instead of thinking holistically, the tendency is to get into survival-mode thinking (lizard brain) or play the politics, fit in at all costs, and avoid pain (monkey brain). How many parents do you know who teach their children to be tough, because it's a dog-eat-eat world out there (lizard brain). I know I have done that, and then it dawned on me that even though my children need to know how to survive in a highly-competitive world, the better way to prepare them is to use their entire brains and have their divine brains be their dominant brains. Teach them to figure out how to contribute instead of just compete. Teach them to serve instead of just fit in. Teach them how to value differences instead of being critical because of differences. The importance of being divinative cannot be overemphasized. Choose to be divinative and you will realize the person you want to be. Choose otherwise and you will fall short of your potential. Decide that your divine brain will be your dominant brain. Resolve that your intent is to live according to the person you want to be. Intent means you intend to follow through on this commitment.

Our hearts and minds are like a patch of fertile soil—something will grow whether we deliberately plant a garden or do little to nothing and allow weeds to multiply. We either develop strength of character or leave it to chance. Leaving it to chance may result in a lack of character.

> **Question:** How are change, improvement, and results achieved, and how do you align your time to consistently develop your character and achieve your goals?
>
> **Answer:** With the use of the Achievement Cycle, beginning with the good or bad results you want to analyze, go in the counter-clockwise direction until you identify the voice that you are listening to, which is at the root of all of your achievements or bad results. The strength and direction of the voice that you listen to is the sum of the strength and direction of your internal voice and external voice. To increase your achievements, align the internal and external voices to which you listen according to the voice of character. When you have completed the counter-clockwise journey, and before you begin the clockwise change, pause to consider: *What do I really want?* Resolve and desire to do what is right, and be the person you want to be. As with a new season commencing with the winter solstice, be divinative, and let your divine light shine ever brighter. Proceed in the clockwise direction, beginning with your voice of character and make the appropriate changes. Continue to spring forward and pre-forgive yourself, resolving to think differently and feel differently. As the summer represents great activity and possibilities, be diligent

and resolve to do and say what is right. Act with integrity. As you go through this process, you will have a great harvest of achievement in the autumn, and you will look at this cycle and season with thanksgiving.

To-Be Action Plans from the Allegory of the Four Seasons

- Go through the Achievement Cycle a number of times, and prove its validity while examining your life and others' lives as well.
- As you examine your life, if your achievements are not what you want them to be, then reexamine your life through this model, and change.
- If you do like your achievements, then reinforce them through this model and continue.

CHAPTER ELEVEN

ALLEGORY #5:
FIVE GOLDEN RINGS

FROM the lesson of the allegory of the three-combination lock, we know
we are trying to balance three lives:

1) Our personal or unseen lives
2) Our private or family lives
3) Our public lives or our lives in the community at large

To unlock and unleash our individual potential, the most effective way to
improve and change is to learn from without, meaning learning from other
people's triumphs and successes. We learn from without by understanding
and following the Achievement Cycle. This is the lesson taught by the allegory of the four seasons. We diagnose our lives or someone else's life, by
moving counterclockwise in the Achievement Cycle, using achievements as
our starting point. We then make the appropriate changes in our lives by
moving clockwise in the Achievement Cycle. The most critical piece of the
Achievement Cycle is listening to and developing the inner voice of character.
From our character will flow what we think and feel, which impacts what we
say and do, which will then lead to our achievements.

So now that we have covered how to learn from without, the next step is
to take what we have learned from others and grow from within. The question this brings up, however, is how to make sure we have a large enough
reservoir of character strength when we need it, instead of finding ourselves
lacking at critical times, and perhaps resorting to lizard-brain or monkey-
brain thinking. It would be beneficial and advantageous to develop character

such that we can apply what we have learned not just to our own lives, but as part of our legacies. When I mention legacy, I'm referring to helping those in our family and in the community at large. In short, how do we continually grow outward (according to our three-combination lock allegory) from our personal lives to our family lives, and even to the community at large?

The development of character parallels the process of finding, producing, and ultimately making use of gold. The five golden rings refer to the five processes needed to make use of gold. The development of our character is also a five-part process. The first three revolve around developing ourselves. The last two parts of developing our character involve applying and strengthening our character development in two areas—the home and the community at large. The parallel steps are;

- Prospecting
- Mining
- Extracting
- Refining
- Use

The final step (Use) depends on the use of the gold, whether for jewelry, in the circuitry of a computer, in surgical instruments, or a myriad of other uses.

Prospecting

Gold is present in almost all rocks and soil, but in most instances it is in such small quantities that it is invisible to the naked eye. Only in those areas where the concentration is large enough, is it profitable to mine gold. Scientists, sometimes referred to as prospectors, look for areas where there are higher concentrations of gold—enough to take the next step—mining.

Similarly, when we consider character traits we wish to develop, all of them exist in every person. All of the wonderful character traits mankind has ever had exist within each of us, to varying degrees. With each individual, like the gold in soils and rock, metaphorically speaking, different character traits are in great abundance, while other character traits are invisible to the naked eye. You may recognize that *compassion*, for example, exists in great abundance and concentration within one individual, and exists in less visible quantities within another individual. Regardless, compassion is there. Certainly all character traits are worth mining, so to speak, but we want to work on those traits that we have in the greatest abundance and purity.

Let's go back to the prospecting of gold. Sometimes when prospectors find deposits of gold, it is indeed pure gold. In most of the gold deposits, however, gold is combined with other metals such as silver. It requires further investigation to determine the amount of gold that exists in the area. When these gold deposits are found, scientist will drill down below the surface, gather samples, and analyze further to decide whether the amount of gold present is worth the effort to mine.

Much as gold can be found in purity in some cases, but combined with other metals most of the time, so are our character traits. They are intermingled. For example, the character trait of *charity* more than likely is connected with the character traits of *service* and *empathy*. This is a wonderful thing, because as we give focus on developing one character trait, we can't help but build other character traits as a natural byproduct.

Our initial effort is in figuring out which character trait to work on first. Choosing character traits to focus on first isn't intended to limit us, but it's simply intended to select our strongest character traits to build a foundation. Ask yourself which character traits are worth your time and effort to mine, refine, and ultimately use first. There are a couple of tests we can do, much as the prospectors drill down and analyze, to choose their priorities. The first suggestion is to think of character traits in people whom you admire and would want to emulate in your own life. There are certain qualities we admire in others, because with some, we see those same traits already in ourselves. We just want to magnify them or bring them closer to our lives. Just as prospectors sometimes need to look below the surface of the earth to find high concentrations of gold, so we need to look more deeply and introspectively. However, we already know (don't we?) in our hearts of hearts, what we can be (as it relates to character) even if others don't know. There are some character traits you may have carefully hidden from others. Those hidden traits need to come out to bless your life and contribute to those around you.

Another suggestion would be to solicit the help of your advisory board that was mentioned in the allegory of the oxen pull. Soliciting the help of your advisory board is analogous to scientists gathering samples to analyze the concentration of gold. Your advisory board members have enough samples of your strongest character traits that they have gathered about you over the years. Ask them. You may not choose to ask all of them, but there are those with whom you can comfortably have a frank conversation about your character traits. You will find that as you ask multiple members of your advisory board, you will hear patterns and recurring themes that will let you know where your greatest strengths lie and what your strongest character traits are. You may have a tendency to be shy about your character traits, and especially if one of them is *humility*. Identifying your character traits is not about being prideful, but it's about "learning from without" sufficiently so that you may grow from within. It's ultimately not just about building a culture of being more personally, but also about knowing the best way to contribute to your loved ones and to humanity. In that spirit, after you have drilled down and done your analysis, what are those character traits that you would want to refine to pure gold?

Write a few of them down.

_____

_____

_____

You cannot get this exercise wrong, because as gold is sometimes mixed with other precious metals such as silver, so is one character trait connected to another. Picking a few character traits to focus on doesn't make them mutually exclusive. Also, remember that this is just one pass at this, but you can go through this exercise as many times as you want. As you identify the character traits that are in abundance within you, celebrate them. Seriously! You are a person of great worth who has much to contribute to others. You have been endowed with these character traits, and they can become a blessing to others, much the same as the character traits you admire in others have strengthened and continue to strengthen you. As you celebrate your strengths, make a "note to self." *Continue being* _____ (insert character traits). The celebration of your character traits is not just a good idea but a critical step of this process, and that celebration can't be skipped. The more you look at your strengths, the more grateful you will be for your uniquenesses. Ask yourself the following questions:

- What are my strongest character traits? (Select at least three.)
- In what ways have they been manifest in my life?
- In what ways have they been a blessing to others?
- How do I feel when I act in accordance to these character traits?
- When I act in accordance to this character trait, what motivates me to act that way?

The reason for examining yourself this way is not just to get an appreciation for your strengths, but to have a personal experience with your heart and mind (remember the distance between heaven and hell section of this book), as to what it feels like to have your character traits appreciated. Remember the third allegory of the three-combination lock? Learn from without, then grow from within. As we grow outward from within, only after we go through the process of appreciating and truly celebrating our strengths and genuinely know from experience what that feels like, can we help our family members and then others see the character traits within themselves. You need to know how to receive before you can know how to give. You will discover how to help others mine their golden character traits and celebrate their strengths once you have recognized your own. This is the essence of the first part of building character.

Identify your strengths or character traits, celebrate them, and continue living according to them. The development of our character starts by being and doing what we already know we should be and do, consistently.

It is all too common and so easy in our time management rush of "doing" stuff, to forget to tap into the character traits that will help us achieve our goals and realize the people we want to be. You may be asking yourself whether magnifying your character traits ultimately leads to achievements. Are there some character traits that are "better" than others? It's not the character traits that matter as much as how we deliberately and consistently apply them that make the difference. The other thing to consider is that your unique combination of character traits may be easier for you to live by and harder for someone else, and vice versa. This is about optimizing *your* character traits and not someone else's.

Mining

Let's go back again to the process of refining gold. Once the prospector has determined there is sufficient gold, he will set up a mining operation. Mining usually involves the use of explosives. Sometimes gold is found close to the surface of the earth, and then open-mine techniques are used. Other times the gold is deeper inside the earth, and underground-mining processes are used. Either way, explosives are used to break up the ground. In parts of the world where explosives are not used or are not available, a great deal of manual labor is required in its stead. The mining process cannot be circumvented. For gold to be of any use, it must be separated from the earth. From the mines, the rocks and soil are then loaded in trucks and hauled to the mill.

The second step in the development of your character requires separation, much as the gold needs to be separated from the earth to be refined. The process of character development may require blowing up your current schedule and taking a completely different approach. It may require a great deal of labor and a coordinated effort from a number of people. It will more than likely require both. Just as the mining process cannot be circumvented from obtaining gold, it is also true that old ways of doing and thinking about time management and character development must be dismissed—and that separation step cannot be bypassed. Blow up these less-than-divine activities that rob you of your time, and replace them with learning to listen to your inner voice of character.

For example, think about your typical week, and think about those activities that are primarily lizard-brain and monkey-brain motivated. Which of those can you reduce, or better yet, altogether eliminate? Some examples of these activities you'd want to reduce or perhaps eliminate might be watching mindless shows on TV, playing computer games endlessly, or surfing the Internet. These are monkey- brain type activities that feel good at the moment but do not lead you towards being the person you want to be. Other activities that can use more scrutiny are some of your e-mails, getting pulled into the latest office or neighborhood drama, phone calls that you know need to get cut off, but you don't know how to tactfully end. Remember, early in the book we talked about the all-you-can-eat buffet and how life is filled with so many choices that one of the important lessons we all must learn is to discern when to say *no* and to what things we will say *no—selective neglect*.

If we are going to develop our character, our lives cannot remain as they are, unexamined and unchanged. Remember that the reason for examining and improving character stems from the understanding that the results and achievements we get in life are a function of how our character meets the challenges we face.

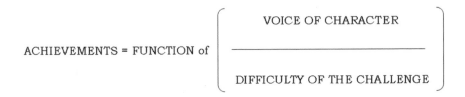

$$\text{ACHIEVEMENTS = FUNCTION of} \left(\frac{\text{VOICE OF CHARACTER}}{\text{DIFFICULTY OF THE CHALLENGE}} \right)$$

The more difficult the challenge, the greater the character required. The greater the results that we want to achieve, again the greater the character needed. This separation we are referring to requires leaving behind what is not needed and taking up what is imperative. Another word closely related to *separation* in the context of building our character is *sacrifice*. The root of the word sacrifice is *sacred*. Sacrifice entails letting go. My intent in mentioning separation and sacrifice is to identify the next step to the development of our character, and it is a very common process for all of us. Anytime we sacrifice or let something go, what remains is more sacred. It is more sacred, because we have paid a price for it. Even something as simple as giving a kind word, writing a "thank-you" note, or a "just-because" letter to a loved one entails sacrificing our time, effort, thought, and attention. What will remain—the words, letter, and the relationship—are more sacred. Think back to when you cared for someone who was sick, and you gave of yourself, your time, and your love. After your service and sacrifice, you were changed, and your soul felt better.

Consider your own experience when you excelled and grew as a person. When you participated in sports or band or any other extracurricular activities in high school, for example, didn't you make sacrifices? Instead of taking an afternoon nap or hanging out with friends after school, you were separated from the comforts of your bed or from the camaraderie of friends, and you had practice. In addition to practice after school, you probably put in additional hours to improve on your own, which may have required some practice on the weekends. It meant even more separation and sacrifice. When the price you paid in practice translates to a win in a sporting event or a great performance, the accomplishment is more meaningful or sacred.

The second step in the development of our character requires sacrifice. Developing the character trait of *love*, for example, may require the sacrifice of letting go of prejudices and truly listening and understanding the other person. It may require forgiveness. This requires subordinating our lizard-brain and monkey-brain thoughts of vengeance and letting go of the pain from being offended.

To err is human, to forgive divine.

—Alexander Pope

Developing the character trait of love may require pre-forgiveness and always seeing the divine in ourselves and others. Sacrificing lizard-brain and monkey-brain thinking may be required. Mining the character trait of love may require the sacrifice of greater thoughtful service. It may require getting out of our comfort zones.

As a simple example, every year I struggle with what to get my wife for Christmas, Valentine's Day, our wedding anniversary, or her birthday. Just for some context, I would struggle to know what to get even for myself, much less for my wife. It requires a great deal of effort, thought, and sacrifice to get the appropriate gift or even to get a letter written. So every year I have built-in occasions to build my character. You probably have similar opportunities as well. In any case, the mining of character requires sacrificing whatever is needed to give us the opportunity to refine our character. The opposite is to get lazy and try to find the most efficient way out. This isn't about speed, but character building. Take the time to give of yourself generously. Selfishness is something else that may need to be sacrificed or separated from our hearts and minds.

Each of these five steps is progressive in nature. Just as prospecting precedes mining, identifying your strongest character traits precedes sacrifice. After identifying a character trait that you want to magnify, the next natural step in character development is to go above and beyond what you are already doing through sacrifice.

I can't imagine a more worthwhile undertaking than the development of your character. It prepares you to get the results and achievements you want. It does, however, take time and focus. Remember one of the foundational realities is the all-you-can-eat buffet analogy or selective neglect. Just as you can't eat everything that is available in an all-you-can-eat buffet every day, you can't do everything there is to do. Give yourself permission to let go of the pursuit of endless *doing*. You have to give character development a high enough priority and take the time to work on it. You have to make deliberate choices and decide what you will selectively neglect. Excellence in any endeavor requires sacrifice and separation; it is no different in the development of excellence in our character.

Extracting

The third step in the gold refining process is called extracting. Remember, the first step is prospecting or finding where the gold concentration is high enough to go to the next step—mining. Mining is separating the gold from the earth and taking it to the mill. Extracting is what happens in the mill. It is a complex process. First the rocks are crushed to the size of gravel and then crushed again to powder. The powder then goes through a series or screens, and chemical solvents are used in the extracting process, so what remains is mostly gold.

The third step in the character development process is learning. Just as gold goes through a myriad of steps to separate everything from the gold, character development goes through a purifying process involving activities such as studying, pondering, reflecting, meditating, reading, and even journal writing. Through these efforts, you will learn and unlearn what is necessary to build your character. This is a very private and personal exercise, and each person will learn and unlearn in his own unique way. What is common in the end, however, is making a commitment to live more fully according to natural laws—and more specifically, living out our strongest character traits more fully. The allegory of the tree included the need for prayer and meditation as well as studying the scriptures and other inspirational literature. The intent there was to assist in helping your divine brain become the dominant brain. The learning that we are speaking of here is a continuation of that development. My experience has been that as I read, I feel that I am getting tutored on the changes and adjustments I need to make to be a better person. Even though I may have read certain passages many times over the years, I glean new meaning each time as my mind and heart are prepared to learn them anew.

> None of us will ever accomplish anything excellent or commanding except when he listens to this whisper which is heard by him alone.
>
> —Ralph Waldo Emerson

Learning Process

As I have observed those who make a serious commitment to learning any field of endeavor, especially learning to build their character, they go through a similar learning process.

1. **Study:** As best as you can, study and absorb as much as you can about the character trait you want to develop.
2. **Teach:** The best way to know how much you have learned thus far and to assess the level of your mastery in any content is to teach it over and over again. Each time you teach you clarify things in your heart and mind. This would apply if you are trying to learn math as much as if you are trying to learn patience. It also helps to teach to people of different ages. When you try to teach humility for example, it's a different experience trying to teach it to someone who is six, versus someone who is sixteen or someone who is sixty. Try it!
3. **Apply:** There's really no point in learning about developing character, if you don't apply it. Start small. Do a little before you do a lot. After applying what you have learned, start the process again as you learn even more.

For example, let's say I want to know about *integrity*. From studying the word, I know that integrity means to adhere to moral and ethical principles. From its root integer (as in whole numbers in math) to have integrity means to be whole. There's a story of a mother asking Gandhi to tell her son to not eat sugar. Gandhi told them to come back in a week. The family returned, and Gandhi told the boy to not eat sugar. The mother wanted to know why they had to wait a week when he could have told the boy the same thing the week before. Gandhi said that he couldn't tell the boy to stop eating sugar the week before, because Gandhi too was eating sugar. As in this Gandhi story, having integrity means that what we say, do, think, and feel are all the same, and they are integrated.

After studying the word integrity the next steps to our learning process are to teach and apply. With my little research of the word integrity and the Gandhi story to enhance my understanding (study), I could have a family meeting where my job is to share with my family what I have learned about integrity (teach) and make a commitment to them to live with more integrity in a particular area. Perhaps I could make a promise to make sure I show kindness every day to each member of the family (apply).

You can do the first step of learning through study on your own. Make up your mind that your divine brain will be your dominant brain. Be divinative. The influence of lizard-brain and monkey-brain thinking in society is strong, constant, and ubiquitous. Start and end each day with divine-brain thinking. The process of learning is really about developing and utilizing your divine brain the rest of the day. There are many levels involved. It is like an upward spiral. One example we covered is seeing the divine in others. One level of seeing the divine in another might be the ability to forgive. Another level above that may be the ability to forgive and forget. Have you ever forgiven someone but kept a mental file? Do you have a mental database where you keep records of the offenses of another, and when you feel the urge, you pull up the file and remind the other person of her past offenses? Perhaps another level may not be to entirely forget, but at least not be tempted to relive and rehash past sins. Perhaps the level above forgiving and forgetting is pre-forgiving, as we have mentioned. Each of these character traits you choose to focus on will have many levels within of them. The learning we are referring to here is a life-long journey of strengthening our character traits.

The teaching and applying we mentioned, is best done with someone else's help. Remember the allegory of the oxen pull and how we need each other to help pull life's load. Everything you have learned in this book will more likely be applied only with the help of someone else—probably someone from your advisory board.

Consider these statistics from the American Society of Training and Development on the likelihood of achieving your goal.

Probability of Completing a Goal

Hear an idea they like	10%
Consciously decide to adopt the idea	25%
Decide when they will do it	40%
Plan how they will do it	50%
Commit to someone else that they will do it	65%
Have a specific appointment with the person they committed to and give an accounting of their progress	**95%**

As we can see from the data, it is more likely that you will apply what you have learned if you solicit help from an accountability adviser to keep yourself on track. The other important lesson we can glean here is that to help your loved ones stay on track, it is not enough to tell him what to do in such a way that he likes the idea (10 percent probability), but he needs you or someone else to report to and to hold him accountable. Getting to 95 percent likelihood of completing a goal is a matter of being thorough. As we commit to learning from without and growing from within, we are filling our reservoirs of character strength as well as preparing for the next step of our character development—refining.

Refining

The fourth step in producing gold is refining. Refining is the process of removing the last of the impurities so that what remains is 99.9 percent pure gold. The gold is put in a crucible, and the intent is to subject the gold to enough heat that the gold will soften and eventually liquefy. Compounds are then added that would separate whatever impurities remain from the gold. There are uses of gold where higher levels of purity (99.99 percent) are required. The more pure the gold, the more intense is the refining process, the higher its value becomes, and the more specialized are its uses.

The parallel to the refining of gold as it relates to building character occurs in the crucible of the home. The third step of building character is learning; this is primarily a mental exercise—though it is an important and necessary step. The refining that occurs in the home takes our learning and gives us experience. It elevates our learning by taking it to the "real world." It doesn't get any more real than in the home. Just as the crucible is a container designed so the gold remains, until it is poured out, so is your family a contained organization. It can prepare all of us and keep us in a purer state. It readies us to be used in many ways.

As a manager, I would use a rigorous hiring process to make sure the person hired had the highest likelihood of succeeding in the end and can contribute significantly to the organization. Most of the time, everything worked great, and the people I hired have become life-long friends. There have been times, however, when things didn't work out, and eventually we parted ways. I then hired someone else. In the home, on the other hand, such is not the case. With our children, there is no interviewing process. It takes a couple of years before newborns can even walk and talk, although they can cry immediately. With children, you get who you get, and each comes with his own divine gifts and talents, as well as human frailties. Shortly after my wife and I brought home our firstborn, it became apparent to me very quickly that we were woefully outnumbered. There were only two of us, and there was a whole wonderful one of her. She didn't come with an instruction manual, return policy, warranties, or money-back guarantee. This parenting thing was strictly on-the-job training, and it would be nothing like I had ever experienced before. Everything before was theoretical. This was the real world in every sense of the word.

In the real world of the workplace, a person can be fired or laid-off. The company can choose to use temporary labor or outsource what they need. It's efficient, logical, and we can always reverse decisions if it's not working out. Not so at home. We all enter the world in a crucible called a family. Like the crucible used to refine gold, our families come in different sizes, styles, and material. What crucibles have in common is the ability to withstand a lot of heat. The structure of the family is designed for the refining of our character. There is no going around. The only way is through. We can't get fired, laid-off, outsourced, or be a temp in a family. Once someone becomes a member of the family, he will always be a member of the family. Not death, divorce, disowning, time, distance, nor absenteeism can completely sever the family ties. The family links may be weak but never severed. In the crucible of the family, our characters can become pure gold. Usually when the word *crucible* is used as a metaphor, it is associated with pain. The crucible of the family, however, can and should be a wonderful thing. Though there can be tough times at home, refining takes place in the process of figuring out how to become a better family. In the heat of challenges, trials, triumphs, laughter, tears, experiences, and how we respond to them, we can realize how much we are growing and how much we are getting refined.

The complete emotional, physical, mental, and spiritual focus that is required in the crucible of the home is the reason why the role of the mother (of course father as well) exceeds the role of an executive in its demands and rewards. When I speak of *reward* I am speaking of the reward of the development of our character. When we are refined in the crucible of the home, we are so much more prepared for any crucible that any of our other roles may present.

> To put the world right in order, we must first put the nation in order; to put the nation in order, we must first put the family in order; to put the family in order, we must first cultivate our personal life; we must first set our hearts right.
>
> —Confucius

I'm not suggesting that everything has to be perfect at home before you do anything else outside the home, because every person has to the ability to choose. Some family members may make wise choices and others not so wise, regardless of what you do. The question is whether or not you are individually doing your part to contribute to the culture you want in your home. Just as an assayer can test gold ores for composition and value, so we can test the strength of our character by how well we are living out our values in our homes. Our homes will reveal to us what it is that we really believe and how much we have really learned. Our homes provide constant and immediate feedback regarding our character.

Remember the distance between heaven and hell and how heaven is having alignment between our hearts and minds. Remember the first three stages:

1) Identifying our strongest character traits and consistently being and doing what we already know we should be and do

2) Making the necessary sacrifice to more consistently live according to character and natural laws

3) Learning through diligent study

All of these involve learning primarily with the mind. Applying what we have learned about character development in the crucible of the home is learning with the heart. I hope you can appreciate how thorough this process is; our divine brains will be tutored well. When we add to our character development the refinement that can be best taught in the crucible of the home, then not only is the divine brain taught, but the heart is taught as well. There are certain life lessons that can only be taught within the walls of our homes. When our hearts and minds learn together at home, in the development of character, we can have a bit of heaven on earth. When you think of time management, isn't this a greater vision than merely increasing the number of things we can get done in a to-do list? Again, our purpose is to pilot our lives to a culture of being more and not just doing more.

In the allegory of the combination lock, to this point we have explored learning from without and two-thirds of growing from within. We have understood growing in our personal and unseen lives, and now we have explored growth in our private or family lives. We'll examine growing in our public lives next. Like the three-combination lock that won't unlock, if we don't succeed in family life, we can't reach our full potential. There will always be that void. It's analogous to getting two of the three numbers in the combination lock right—close but not quite there. If you are doing everything you can to create the culture you want in your home, but it's not quite there yet, be divinative, smile a lot, stay in divine-brain mode, and just stay the course. If you need to make changes, or make mistakes along the way, pre-forgive yourself, and get back on course. Allow the heat from the crucible of the home to remove any remaining impurities and refine your heart and mind.

Using Gold

Once the gold is refined, the next step depends on how the gold will be used. Let's pause here for a little bit and take an inventory of what we have explored thus far, and look at the commitments you are considering making.

- Be divinative. Have your divine brain be your dominant brain. Its intelligence, compared to the lizard brain and monkey brain, is as brilliant as the light of the noon-day sun compared to the moon and stars.

- Commit to piloting your life towards a culture of being more, and not just doing more.
- See and treat time as opportunity measured in units of possibilities.
- Shift your thinking from individual performance to contributing to others. (Clark Kent to Superman).
- Align what you feel in your heart with what you know your mind. (Distance between heaven and hell).
- Selectively neglect some of your activities. You can't do everything all the time. (Remember the all-you-can-eat buffet comparison).
- Have a defense against the fires of your life that come from without as well as the diseases that comes from within. (Allegory of the tree—Bristlecone Pine and Redwood tree)
- Make a commitment to repeatedly go through the growing pains in the Zigzag Path to Growth, even if it doesn't feel good at the moment. It will, however, feel great later, as you get ever closer to realizing your mission.
- Commit to prayer or meditation and studying scriptures or other inspirational material as you begin and end your days in the divine-brain mode.
- See the need to work with others and lift each other's load. (Allegory of the oxen pull).
- Pre-forgive yourself so you can pre-forgive others, and keep yourself in the divine-brain mode.
- Assemble your advisory board.
- Keep in mind that you have three lives; your personal life, your private or family life, and your public life or your life in the community at large. Remember they are all important. This is the allegory of the three-combination lock.
- Approach change and improvement by learning from without and growing from within.
- Analyze and approach goal achievement through the Achievement Cycle. (Allegory of the four seasons).

- Identify your strongest character traits, and be consistent in being and doing what you already know you should be and do.
- Make the necessary sacrifices of yourself and of your time to develop your character.
- As the world-class musician, athlete, or scholar with a strict regimen, makes the necessary sacrifices and is also a student of her craft, commit to learning and improving.
- Apply to your home what you have learned in the building of your character.
- Like painting a masterpiece one brush stroke at a time, commit to consistently make small improvements that will help you be the person you want to be.
- Commit to other insights you have gained as a result of these allegories.

Wow! As you deliberately and progressively follow through on these commitments, you are prepared to make any contribution you want to make. You are pure gold. The allegory of the golden rings is about building character. It is interesting to note that when you look at the history of the word *character*, it comes from the 14th century Greek word "kharakter," which means an engraved mark. Gold is a soft metal, which makes it easier to engrave, compared to other harder metals. As we all go through the character-purifying process of identifying character traits that we want to emulate in our lives, being and doing what we already know we should (prospecting), making the necessary sacrifices to focus and improve further (mining), diligently learning and unlearning to elevate our understanding (extracting), and applying our character in the crucible of the home (refining), our hearts and minds will be sufficiently softened, allowing us to then engrave upon them the character traits that we want to live by. Such softening and the engraving of both our character and confidence onto our beings, will prepare us to make the kind of contributions we want to make to society. If, on the other hand, we are hard-headed or hard-hearted, engraving anything new on our hearts and minds may prove to be a difficult task. As a parent or executive, have you ever found it difficult to help someone change her character? It's because she was too hard-headed and hard-hearted. There's no way around but to go through a process of softening both the heart and mind.

Here's another interesting tidbit. Consider a thin strip of metal like tin, for example. As you bend it back and forth, eventually the strip of metal will break in two. It is also the case when gold is worked, even though it is a softer metal. With gold, however, if you reheat and liquefy it through the refining process, the gold can regain its soft and moldable state again. Similarly, whenever you find yourself getting worked and hardened by the challenges of your day-to-day activities and feel as if you might break, keep going back to this character development process, from revisiting and being grateful for your strengths and character, to spending time and effort getting refined in the crucible of your home, and you will find that you can be softened again, have the engraved mark of character imprinted deeper in your soul. Then you can continue to make your unique contributions.

Being able to contribute in a significant way requires not just that our hearts and minds be aligned, but add to that a feeling of *stewardship*. When you look at people who have made significant contributions in their lives, they are people with great character, ability, and passion. Not only did they feel strongly about their causes, but they had the faith and ability to impact those causes, and they felt that tug or that call that says they are here on earth for that purpose. In a conversation with a friend, I asked him if he has discovered his life's calling. He replied, "Oh yeah, I got the call. I just put it on hold." As you go through this fifth allegory of the five golden rings, you will get a sense of the engraving of your character, and as you do, you will hear your call more audibly in your heart and mind—the unique contribution you need to make. Don't put your life's calling on hold; answer it.

> Success is not built on what we accomplish for ourselves. Its foundation lies in what we do for others.
>
> —Danny Thomas

Back to using gold. Gold is generally too soft for practical use, so other metals are generally added to it. For example, some prefer white gold over yellow gold for jewelry. White gold is made by combining nickel or silver with the gold. Red or pink gold is an alloy combining gold with copper. Likewise, having a great character is not enough. Being competent in your field of work needs to be added to make a contribution. Being competent in a particular discipline combined with weak character is what fills the evening news with people who were once held up as role models, but are now criminals. Strong character with insufficient competence is also not enough. They are the wonderful people of the world who never seem to get the right breaks, get frustrated, and wonder whether having high character is worthwhile.

Balancing great character with great competence gives us great confidence. Having both enables us to make contributions and allows us to impact others in significant ways. Remember the Achievement Cycle in the allegory of the four seasons. We begin with the achievements we want. We identify the character traits we need to draw from. From there we develop and align our thoughts and feelings. Getting the results and achievements we want, requires the cultivation of our minds and talents. In a global economy and with change happening at an accelerated rate, part of your time needs to be allotted to the development of your mind.

Learning is a treasure that will follow its owner everywhere.
—Chinese Proverb

Like combining other metals to gold to create a usable alloy, combining character with competence allows us to make significant contributions. As we have done with the previous allegories, let's take a look at the question this allegory is supposed to answer.

Question: Where and how do I start in my quest to develop my character?

Answer: After establishing a strong desire to develop you character, commit to the following process that parallels the refining and use of gold.

- **Prospecting:** Identify your strongest character trait and continue to live by it.
- **Mining:** Make the necessary sacrifices so you can make time to focus on the development of your character.
- **Extracting;** Study and learn to make your strengths even stronger.
- **Refining;** Diligently apply your character strength in your home.
- **Use of Gold:** Apply your character strength in all your roles.

These same processes are used to achieve excellence in anything. Think of someone who has excelled and is the very best in her field, whether that is in the arts, music, sports, or any profession. Can you see how he or she has applied the following steps in an effort to master her craft?

- He is diligent in what he knows he should already be doing (Prospect).
- He sacrifices and reallocates his time to make a concerted effort and focus toward improving (Mine).
- He is constantly learning and he is a student of his craft (Extract).
- She is committed to those relationships that will help her to excel (Refine)
- She goes beyond sacrifice and gives her full devotion to bless the lives of others (Use of Gold).

CHAPTER TWELVE

ALLEGORY #6: ACHIEVING FLIGHT

WE have been engaged in a significant journey thus far, exploring concepts to pilot our lives towards a culture of being more and not just doing more. These are important ideas, and I'm sure you have added to it your own insights and wisdom. We haven't forgotten, however, that this is about time management, and we need to have the rigor to consistently apply what we have learned. Events such as reading this book alone may fade, but creating a process with it enables our learning to endure. Our last allegory is about application.

Every time I fly, I love getting the window seat on the plane and looking out as the plane takes off. It's especially exciting when I'm on the largest planes. I can feel the power of the engines as the plane accelerates down the runway. Although I have flown over a million miles, the idea that man can and does fly is fascinating and exciting to me. Soon after the plane is off the ground, the plane retracts the landing gear, and then without the drag of the landing gear, the flight is smoother and becomes quieter. All the while, the plane continues to lift and rise above the trees, buildings, hills, and even the highest mountains. As the plane steadily climbs, my vision expands. I especially love the morning and afternoon flights when it is cloudy and even rainy. The plane climbs through the rain and clouds and then suddenly breaks through the mist of gray into the glorious sunshine. The plane continues to climb through occasional turbulence, then finally there is a smooth flight, with the feeling of perfect stillness, and I look out the plane window with unlimited visibility.

It is amazing how the take-off on a commercial flight parallels our own lives. We want our lives to take flight, and we want to position ourselves much as the plane positions itself on one end of the runway with a flight plan established. It takes a tremendous effort just to get a plane moving and gaining speed in preparation for flight. So it is with us. Resolve, effort, and persistence are required, along with our personal flight plan or mission. Daily uplifting habits are pre-requisites for us to gain momentum and lift. Much as the miracle of commercial flight happens daily, so can we have the hope within us and the example of others who have gone before, to soar to heights that we may only currently hold with faith. Just as adherence to the laws of flight dictates whether or not the plane will lift above clouds, darkness, and storms, and arrive at its destination, so are we assured that we can become the people we want to be, regardless of the storms we have to weather, when we understand and adhere to the laws that lift men's souls. We'll explore in four sections this allegory of achieving flight.

- Flight Plan or Mission Statement
- Accelerating down the runway and lift
- Adjustments along the way
- Putting it all together with a simple and powerful tool

Flight Plan or Mission Statement

Just as a plane doesn't leave the airport until the pilot has a destination and flight plan, we also need our personal flight plan or personal mission statement. There are many ways to do a mission statement. The correct and great mission statement is the one in which you can answer *yes* for this question: *Does it inspire me?* I've seen personal mission statements as long as twelve pages and as short as two words. I've seen mission statements in which there were no words, because they had captured their mission statements through art, music, or objects. A personal mission statement is indeed very personal. Make it however you would like, so long as it is inspiring to you. A personal mission statement is something you revisit regularly and change as your life's experience and insights change.

For your first draft of your mission statement, however, consider the following approach. Your first draft will have four parts. They are:

- The character traits you want to cultivate and emulate in your life
- The goals and achievements you want for yourself
- The culture you want to create in your family
- The contribution you want to make to the community at large through your work life, family life, volunteer work, and any other roles you may have

That's it! Keep it that simple. Again, you'll probably revise it over time, and that's okay, but this four-part first draft of your mission statement will give you a great start. I first wrote my first mission statement about eighteen years ago, and it has undergone some revisions. My mission statement, based on my experience and estimation, is probably 85 percent complete. I'm not worried about my mission statement being 100 percent complete right away, as much as I am excited about being the type of person I want to be and living my life accordingly. I'll make changes to my mission statement as I see fit. It inspires me. It's my personal flight plan, and I am excited to travel towards it. Your mission statement will also inspire you. So let's get started on your first draft of your personal mission statement!

Cultivate Character. What are at least three character traits you want to live by? You wrote down a few to consider on page 104.

_____

_____

_____

_____

Identify the personal goals and personal achievements you want just for you. If you were the last person left on earth, what personal goals would you set just for your personal satisfaction?

_____

_____

_____

_____

Create Family Culture. From your gut, what do you want your family culture to be like?

_____

_____

_____

Contribute to Community. With your unique talents, gifts, and interests, what are the contributions that you would like to make at work, in your community, in your church, and in other roles you may have?

_____

_____

_____

_____

When you consider and ponder these questions, and then give your sincere answers—congratulations! You have finished your first draft of your mission statement. Consider what each of these four questions mean. As you thought about all of these questions, you were in divine-brain mode. In answering these four questions, you have considered your three lives that we mentioned in the allegory of the three-combination lock: your personal or unseen life, your private or family life, and your public life or your life in the community at large.

By answering the first question about character traits, you identified the voice of your trainer that we explored in the allegory of the oxen pull. These may have even coincided with the character traits you chose on page 104. By thinking deeply about the first question, you answered the most critical piece in the allegory of the four seasons and the Achievement Cycle—the character traits you want to live by.

When you answer the second question, you will express, by your personal goals and achievements, the unique you. You will lift yourself, which is the only way you will have the strength to lift others.

By answering the third question, you are on your way to your personal refining process that we discussed in the allegory of the five golden rings. You are being refined and purified in the crucible of the home.

By answering the fourth question, you are aware of the unique contribution you can make that would give you an additional sense of fulfillment and contribution. As you implement your mission statement, you'll see the allegory of the tree come to fruition. You'll have the defense from the fires that come into your life from without, and you will also have a strong immune system to fight disease from within. You'll find continued success for a long time.

Accelerate Down the Runway and Lift

Once you have a flight plan or have at least the first draft of your mission statement, it's time to accelerate down the runway and lift off. Accelerating down the runway of your life towards the flight plan of your mission statement requires committing to the Zigzag Path to Growth that we explored earlier. There will be times when you feel great and other times when you don't feel so great. Regardless, focus on your mission or flight plan, and know that growing pains are simply part of your growth process. There will be hard moments, and you may feel at times that you would rather stay in bed and pull the covers over your head, but that feeling quickly fades, and you muster the courage to keep going. There may be occasional storms and turbulence in your ascent towards your mission, but don't fret, because those events are as common to man as are storms and turbulence in a commercial flight.

ZIGZAG PATH TO GROWTH

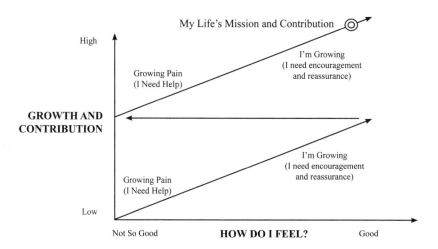

The hard moments in trying to achieve flight involve a pair of opposing forces—lift versus weight and drag versus thrust. The force of weight or gravity is always present, and creating lift to fly requires effort. We'll identify and examine those things that weigh us all down as well as looking at specific strategies to lift ourselves and fly towards our mission. Thrust is what moves the plane forward and drag slows the plane down. The forces of lift, weight, thrust, and drag are constantly in play during flight, and they each need to be managed. Similarly, we are trying to manage those same types of forces within our own lives.

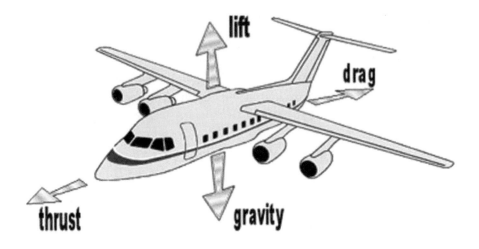

The word *lift* refers to the power to rise to a new level or altitude. In aerodynamics, when the pressure underneath the wings of a plane is greater than pressure over the wing, then lift occurs. When the skyward lift is sufficient to overcome the downward pull of gravity, the plane takes flight. When we are trying to lift our lives, we are actually trying to lift four areas:

1) Our personal lives expressed through character
2) Our personal lives expressed through the mind and body
3) Our relationships expressed in our family lives or private lives
4) Our relationships expressed through our public lives or our lives in the community at large

In these four areas it's important to understand equally what lifts us up and moves us forward in these areas, as well as to identify those things that weigh us down and create drag in our lives.

Lifting Your Character

Throughout most of the world a great emphasis has been placed on the importance of formal education. Families, corporations, and governments alike recognize that the health and progress of a nation and indeed the world are affected by the improvement of the mind. Our standard of living is better because of technology and innovation born of education. There is also growing information in the realm of emotional intelligence. In Daniel Goleman's book *Emotional Intelligence,* he declares that emotional intelligence redefines what it means to be smart. He presents how emotional intelligence (EQ) can matter more than IQ. When it comes to our physical well-being, there is also much that has been written in the areas of health, exercise, nutrition, medicine, and so forth. We see people living longer than ever. We see athletes who are stronger, bigger, faster, and their careers are lasting longer. We continually make improvements in understanding and combating disease.

Despite all of these advancements, our society still faces the same weaknesses because of character flaws. Such weakness manifests itself when we see greed in our corporations and governments, selfishness in relationships, apathy and indifference towards the suffering of others, feelings of insecurity and hopelessness, violence—basically lizard-brain and monkey-brain behavior. Character development like other intelligences requires our time and attention in order for us to improve.

We'll identify ideas to lift our character. We have covered them, but let's organize them in the context of applying them in the allegory of flight and in our time-management tool that we will cover at the end of this chapter.

- Be Divinative
- Pre-forgive Yourself
- Prospect, Mine, and Extract Your Character Traits

Be divinative. Begin and end your day with prayer or meditation as well as scripture study or reading inspirational literature. If you look at one of the reasons why some organizations are better than others, it is because they have something that distinguishes them and makes them unique compared to others. Similarly, if we are going to improve, we need to have insights that we didn't have before. Beginning and ending your day with divinative activities lends itself to gaining more insights. Why would this be the case? Because you are more likely be in an "insight reception" mode when you pray or meditate first thing in the morning and as you ponder on the day you just had during the evening, as opposed to being in a to-do list mode as soon as you wake up. In the past few months of writing this book, for example, I have had an acceleration of personal insights early in the morning. I have received more insights early in the morning than the steady insights I have received from years of experiences that led me to write this book in the first place. Think back on those times when out of the blue you received that flash of brilliance, and you come up with a great idea. Imagine having more of them more often. Commit to beginning and ending your day in the divine-brain mode. What would keep you from being divinative? Procrastination. You might think, "I'll do the divine brain stuff later—right after I do a couple of really pressing things." Resist the temptation to procrastinate. Be divinative first thing in the morning, and have your prayer or meditation time. Depending on the day, you could find yourself beginning your day in crisis mode, and then going from one fire to the next from sunrise to bedtime. Using the flight analogy, it's tough to achieve flight if you are weighed down all day long.

Pre-forgive yourself. When you pre-forgive yourself, you affirm yourself. You remind yourself that you are a person of great worth who deserves patience and another chance. What would weigh us down is being overly critical of ourselves and feeling guilty. Feeling guilty can be a great warning system that tells us to change our course, but when guilt does nothing more than paralyze us, then it is self-defeating.

Prospect, Mine, and Extract. Going back to the allegory of the five golden rings, identify your character strengths, make the necessary sacrifices to develop your strongest character traits, and seek to improve through study and application.

Lifting Your Capabilities

Many people, especially moms, do many things for other people, but not enough for themselves. As they give more and more but don't do anything to lift themselves, they run out of energy to give to others. How long do your laptops, and cell phones last without having their batteries recharged? Metaphorically speaking, it is easy to recognize that you need to recharge your own batteries. The other consideration, however, is defining balance and moderation. How much of lifting yourself is too much, to the point where you feel guilty about perhaps being selfish, and how much is not enough, causing you to feel that you don't have enough of yourself to give to others? I have heard this question asked many times, and it is much more difficult to answer in the context of only lifting yourself. However, when viewed from the standpoint of fulfilling your mission and getting out of the holding pattern you may find yourself in, it is easier to see how you need to simultaneously lift not just yourself, but your character and your family members, as well as lifting others in your other roles.

Increasing your capabilities mirrors the Achievement Cycle we explored in the allegory of the four seasons. We just discussed lifting character, which mirrors the voice of character in our Achievement Cycle. Our voice of character influences what we think and feel. Lifting your capabilities means developing yourself mentally (what we think) and developing ourselves emotionally (what we feel). What we think and feel affects what we do and say, and so we also need to lift ourselves physically. To lift yourself mentally, emotionally, and physically, see the following list of what others do. You may choose from the list, or hopefully the list will trigger other ideas that would be best for you. The key is to be consistent. It's up to you whether you choose one idea to focus on or whether you choose several and change things up a bit for variety.

LIFTING YOURSELF MENTALLY

Read about broad range of topics	Write a book	Learn a new language
Attend classes and workshops	Meditate	Learn a new skill
Do crossword puzzles	Laugh	Memorize poems
Write down goals	Ask questions	Travel
Garden	Take vacations	Reflect
Go to a museum	Scrapbook	Keep a Journal
Experience different cultures	Garden	Paint
Play a musical instrument	Yoga	Care for the elderly
Discover your strengths		
Learn from without grow from within		

Lifting Yourself Emotionally

Organize your advisory board	Build relationships
Visit a friend	Forgive yourself and others
Reach out to neighbors	Laugh
Give positive feedback	Take time to celebrate small successes
Make time to renew friendships	Smile
Pay it forward	Share memories
Travel to understand other cultures	Give random acts of kindness
Think before you speak	Date night with spouse or children
Looking through photos and videos	Compliment others
Volunteer	Call your mom

Lifting Yourself Physically

Exercise	Martial arts	Relaxation
Walk	Drink enough water	Yoga
Run	Get enough sleep	Pilates
Stretching	Focus on your desired weight	Eat a balanced diet
Dance	Get a physical	Play with kids
Join a gym	Walk your dog	Set fitness goals
Ride a bike	Take your vitamins	Hike
Tennis	Golf	Mow the lawn

Again, the key in lifting yourself is to be consistent and know that you are doing this to create a culture of being more and not just doing more. You are lifting yourself, and that is just as important as lifting others. Pick at least one thing from each area that you will commit to doing. It is better to start off very conservatively, because keeping small promises such as lifting yourself will help you make and keep bigger promises to yourself as well as to others.

I will lift myself mentally by:

_____

_____

_____

_____

I will lift myself emotionally by:

_____

_____

_____

_____

I will lift myself physically by:

_____

_____

_____

_____

Lifting Your Family

> There is no doubt that it is around the family and the home that all the greatest virtues, the most dominating virtues of human society, are created, strengthened and maintained.
>
> —Winston Churchill

The following are the highest-leverage activities we can do to lift our family members.

- Help your family to be divinative
- Monitor any early warning signs
- Pre-forgive
- Listen
- Expand their vision with patience
- Words and acts of kindness
- Help your children assemble their advisory boards

Be Divinative. We've certainly covered this topic of being deliberate and definitive in our resolve to have our divine brains be our dominant brains. As we personally see greater benefits from being divinative, the more we will want to share this with our families. Helping someone be more divinative is a wonderful gift to give. However, this is a gift that can only be given after it has been received. Helping others to be more divinative requires us to be divinative first and be a model. Lifting our families by encouraging them to be divinative takes our examples and convictions. It may even require our testimonials that it works. Let your family know the difference that being divinative has made and continues to make in your life when you begin and end each day in the divine-brain mode. Be consistent in asking them if they began and ended their days with prayer or meditation and reading scriptures or uplifting literature. Remember the statistic that if you want to achieve a goal, your probability of achieving that goal rises to 95 percent if you make a firm decision to act, make a time commitment, create a plan, and hold yourself accountable to someone else. To achieve the goal of having your family members be divinative, as the leader in the home, share your decision, commitment, and plan to help each family member be divinative consistently every day. As a leader in the home, allocate some time daily to be responsible for being the person who will help each member of your family be accountable for divine-brain thinking.

How do you do this exactly? First, begin your day with your personal prayer or meditation and reading of scriptures or inspirational literature. Then, having begun your day in the divine-brain mode, ask each member of your family in the morning with a smile, "Have you started your day with your smartest divine brain already going? This may sound cheesy to you, but imagine what it would be like from your children's point if you asked them to do something you had not done, and you asked them with a frown on your face? They would think, *Mom or Dad wants me to do something that they don't look enthused about?* If, on the other hand, they can feel your excitement, and if they can see the difference it is making in you, they will more likely follow your lead. This activity literally only takes a few seconds each day to complete, but it can make a profound difference to you and every member of your family.

Monitor any early-warning sign. In my travels for work, from time to time I find myself in the middle of bad weather patterns. In such travels I have found it a great benefit to find out in the news, early warning signs, whether the dangers that lurk ahead are winter storms or flash floods. In other parts of the world, there may be early warning signs for hurricanes, tsunamis, or tornados. Such warnings allow all of us to prepare for dangers that we may not have expected or could not yet foresee. As you consider your family members, it is also possible to have early warning signs of dangers that you may not have expected or cannot yet see.

As you make it part of your daily routine and time management with your family to read together inspirational literature—whether you are reading the Bible, Bhagavad Gita, Qur'an, Buddhavacana, or Aesop's fables—these are great opportunities to teach about character. It is of equal importance that as you read and learn together as a family, you listen and pay attention to how family members respond and comment on what you are reading. Their comments can provide early-warning signs on those principles where they have questions or are struggling. Inspirational literature teaches us lessons that others have learned in the past. They teach us about success and failure paths that others have taken in the past. The way your family responds to the lessons in inspirational literature will let you know whether they too are headed down success paths or failure paths. If they are headed down success paths as illustrated in your reading, congratulate them and let them know how you are pleased that they are living their lives in much the same way as the wonderful examples you are reading about. If, on the other hand, you discern that they are headed down a failure path, whatever scripture or inspirational literature you are reading, probably will give you helpful insights that you can then highlight. Have the wisdom to listen more than you lecture. Have the courage to speak plainly. In the complex world in which we live, straight talk with love is best. The ability to get early-warning signs of danger about your family members is worth every minute of time you spend to secure it.

Moms tell me that at first the family is excited about these divinative activities, because of the novelty. Within a few days, however, at times the kids just roll their eyes in disbelief that this phase hasn't already passed. Persist. Commit to being consistent for twenty-one days, because it takes about that long to form a habit. Remember, you are helping family members begin and end their days in the divine-brain mode. You are facilitating the building of character, and you are helping them learn to listen to their internal voices of character. Think back to the Achievement Cycle. Our internal voices of character affect how we think and feel, which in turn influences what we do and say, which will determine our achievements. Learning together from scriptures or inspirational literature as a family is such a high-leveraged use of your time.

Pre-Forgive. Along with personally being divinative, we have also covered the notion of pre-forgiving yourself. It is a pre-requisite for you to pre-forgive others, especially those in your family. In a world where criticism, cynicism, and perfectionism are becoming more prevalent than encouragement and the celebration of successes, we need more than ever to be reassured and pre-forgiven. The spirit of pre-forgiveness is seeing the very best in your family members now, as well as seeing the potential in their divine brains for the future. Pre-forgiveness with family members is letting go of those times when they think more with their lizard brains and monkey brains than with their divine brains. It also means continuing to have confidence and faith in the best and the divine in them. As you consider how you manage your time, include pre-forgiving your family members as an area of focus.

Listen. As we go through our planning process, whether for the day or week, we are trying to come up with the activities that would be of greatest worth for us to accomplish. One of the greatest things we can do to lift family members is to truly listen with the intent to understand them more deeply.

When you look at the history and the origin of the word *listen*, you will find that it means to *hear splendor and honor*. Listen also means to *hear glory*. Imagine how our conversations would be different if we listened with the intent to hear splendor, honor, and glory. We would be less inclined to listen with the intent of fixing someone or solving her problems, because we are first trying to appreciate how wonderful she already is. In a training session for teachers that I attended on teaching teenagers, the instructor said in essence:

> If you could fast forward in time and realize who your students have the potential to become and get a glimpse now of what they will eventually accomplish, you would be too intimidated to teach them.

I'm not suggesting living in a Pollyanna world, but simply encouraging all of us to give as much credence to potential as we give to history.

When we bring home a newborn from the hospital, we watch in awe at this beautiful baby. We wonder what her life will be like. We dream of what she can eventually be. In short, we don't worry about her history, because she has none. We only look at her potential. As each year passes, however, the scales slowly tip toward paying ever more attention to history and a little bit less attention to potential. In time, we give what people have done in the past more weight than what they can become in the future. Eventually, there comes a point where we decide that what we see now is all we will ever get in the future. Good or bad, we now have a finished product. In reality, there is plenty of potential left. As long as we live, there are chapters in our lives yet to be written.

Have you ever had someone see you in a better light than you saw yourself? What were they looking at ... just your history? I don't think so. I believe they saw, in equal doses, what you have done in the past and what you can yet do and be. They then focused their attention on what you can be. Imagine driving your car with your front windshield covered, and you drive forward, only looking at your rear-view mirror. Disaster! Similarly, we sometimes try to move forward with our loved ones and work colleagues while only looking backwards. Listen with the intent to hear honor, splendor, and glory. See and focus more on the potential than history of others. You will marvel at the improvement in your relationships as you are deliberate with this skill. Schedule in your planner the time to implement this into your life.

LISTENING WHEN EMOTIONS ARE HIGH

Have you ever had someone come to you, wanting to talk when he was highly emotional? After a few minutes, as you sat frozen in silence, he thanked you and then left. He felt better, and you were left by yourself wondering what had just happened. When this has happened to me, I've often wondered what the person was thanking me for, because I clearly didn't know when he came in, nor when he left, what he was talking about.

When it comes to the use of your time in lifting members of your family, one of the most important skills in building relationships is the ability to listen when the emotions are high. It's much more difficult with a family member than with others, because we are emotionally invested. We bring into the conversation years of experience from the past, and years of concern for the future. Generally speaking, women are much better at this skill. I have seen many who have an almost unconscious competence when it comes to listening with empathy. So for some of you, this may be a good review. For others, it will bring consciousness to your unconscious competence. For others still, it will be your means to help someone else develop listening skills.

Think of a scenario—let's say a highly-emotional teenager. Is he logical or illogical? Is he rational or irrational? More than likely he is both illogical and irrational. He will come to you, and because you have a desire to help, and because you love this teenager, you truly want to understand what is troubling him. The tendency is to want to ask questions. Why do we do that? Because our intent is to want to first understand, and then we can help. After all, how can we help, when we don't even understand the problem? We may think that if we can just get some key information—it doesn't even have to be complete—but enough so that we can process it from experience or others we have known, then we can make some progress. We just need a few helpful hints to help get started. If he can answer your questions, if his comments make logical sense, and if he doesn't become even more emotional, then you're fine, and this strategy will work. If not, change your strategy—immediately.

The problem with this scenario is, the more questions we ask, the more emotional the teenager tends to become. The more emotional he becomes, the more illogical the answers. The more we ask questions to clarify, the more irrational he becomes. The more emotional and illogical and irrational he becomes, the more irritated we become. Sound vaguely familiar? Let's keep going. The more irritated we become, we can sense that we are getting more emotional.

Let's review. The conversation started with an emotional and irrational teenager and a cool, calm, collected parent with no other agenda than to help this child. After a few questions, the teenager's emotional level has escalated, and the parent is headed in the same direction. When the emotion of the parent matches that of the child—folks, that's called a fight! We may have started with intentions to help, and we may end up with name calling. What happened to the listening for splendor, honor, and glory? It gradually disappeared somewhere in the conversation.

Rewind. When the emotions were high with the teenager, and he was irrational and illogical, we were doomed to fail when our intent was to try and understand him. We didn't stand a chance of understanding him, because he didn't understand himself. The situation calls for a different skill-set and mind-set. The mind-set should change from trying to understand him to helping him feel understood. This is worth repeating. Don't try to understand someone who doesn't understand himself. Instead help him feel understood. This requires a few ground rules.

- Don't ask so many questions. He doesn't have the answers.
- Don't give answers. He doesn't know the question.
- Don't tell him whether he is right or wrong. He doesn't know what's up from down, much less what's right or wrong at the moment.

When we listen to someone when emotions are low, usually the active use of the ears and mind is enough. We use the ears to get incoming data, and we use our minds to process the data. When emotions are high, we need to use two more organs above and beyond the mind and the ears. We also need to use the eyes and the heart. We both see and feel what someone is going through. Use your ears, mind, eyes, and heart, and then use your own words to reflect back what is happening.

The skill itself is quite simple, actually. You have used it many times and may not even have realized it. Think back to when you were watching a particular movie at home for the first time, and there was a part of the movie that was sad or tragic. As you were watching these scenes, let's say a friend came into the room and asked you what just happened in the last scene of the movie. I would imagine as you would try to tell your friend what had just happened, that you would intend to be as accurate as possible. You would use words to convey the context, the content, and the feeling. You would translate what had just happened without any judgment. What happened is what happened, and you are just trying to be accurate in your story telling. Listening with empathy is trying to be accurate without any judgment. In trying to convey what is happening in the movie, I can't imagine that you would begin by giving advice or asking questions.

Listening to someone who is emotional is listening with the ears, mind, eyes, and heart. You simply want to reflect back what is happening. Your intent is to help him feel understood. He is not interested in your advice or questions. He is not even interested in having you understand him. He is interested in feeling understood. When you have listened and feel the need to say something, simply convey back to him primarily what your eyes see, and what your heart feels as you would convey to someone else what had just happened in a movie. The more he feels understood, eventually the less emotional he will be. In time, when he is ready and asks for it, you can give advice and ask questions. In the meantime, help him feel understood.

Allow me to give a word of caution here, however. If this skill is used with the wrong intent, the other person will sense it, and you can be in big trouble. The wrong intent is to come in as the problem solver, making the other person feels as if she is getting fixed. The right intent is to truly want to help the person feel understood and have no other agenda.

Help Expand Vision with Patience. In my associations with many parents, as well as in my own experience, there is a tendency to underestimate our children's intelligence and overestimate their experience. Consequently we make certain assumptions about what we thought they should already know, and we're disappointed when they don't act accordingly. These could range from the very pragmatic to the abstract, such as:

- Cleaning their rooms
- Eating etiquette
- Cleaning up their messes
- The value of work
- Understanding that the decisions made today affect the future
- The importance of respecting people's time
- They are judged by their appearance regardless of whether it is right or wrong
- Being respectful to others makes a big difference
- The power to choose, etcetera

John Wooden was the men's basketball coach for UCLA, and in his tenure he won ten NCAA national championships. That is the highest number of men's basketball championships for any coach; the next closest is four. He was also voted the coach of the century for all of sports. One of the first things he would teach his players was how to properly put on their socks and tie their shoes. The players thought it was a childish exercise at first, but he would explain to his players that not putting on your socks and shoes properly could give you blisters, which could affect the quality of your play, and that could negatively affect the outcome of a game. All of his players were talented, and had been playing basketball for many years. Many of them would go on to play at the professional level, but he taught them the basics and expanded their vision of why these and other basics are so important.

Expanding your children's vision and understanding with patience means being more apt to teach, mentor, and coach, than to assume and judge. Ask your kids questions to check their level of understanding. Through asking questions you'll know what parts to skip and what to emphasize. There may be some things they know already, and you just need to do a quick review, but there's no shame in over communicating if they already understand. Don't you wish over communication would happen more often? When kids do something wrong, get in the mode of listening. Then when you have listened sufficiently so that you can hear glory and honor, you can lovingly teach and expand their vision and understanding instead of lecturing. Much like coach

John Wooden explained how putting on shoes and socks correctly can affect the outcome of games, take the time to help your children make the important connections that will help them in their lives. Some connections are harder for them to make, because they have not had the same life experiences you have had. Imagine how uplifting it would be when we make mistakes, if someone would suspend judgment, would take the time to listen, and then expand our vision and understanding. We would feel affirmed, valued, and worthy of someone's time and attention to explain things to us.

What would add weight and drag, using the flight analogy, would be to assume, be impatient, and have a family member feel stupid. You may have even taught the same lesson before. That's okay. Learning requires repetition, and sometimes they, like us, may have taken a mental vacation when we should have been listening. So you may have taught them, but they may not have been listening at those critical moments. Keep teaching, pre-forgiving, and expanding their vision while being patient yourself.

Do Acts and Use Words of Kindness. In the allegory of the four seasons, we mentioned the idea that achievements stem from what we do and from what we say. One of the most important things we can do to lift our families is to use words with them that communicate affirmation, acceptance, and validation. Be quick to compliment. Be quick to point out your family member's character strengths when you see those strengths manifest. Let you family members know that you love them, appreciate them, and are proud of their right decisions. Affirm them as they live their lives down a path that will help them be their best selves.

Help Your Children Assemble Their Advisory Boards. Have you ever been concerned that your children may be spending time with the "wrong" crowd? In your time-management strategy include time to help your children assemble their advisory boards. Share what you have learned in assembling your own advisory board. Tell them what a difference it has made for you. Help them come up with the criteria for choosing members of their advisory boards. As you model for your children what it means to be divinative, to be pre-forgiving, to listen, to speak words of kindness and affirmation, and as you expand their vision with patience, you will strengthen your relationship with them. With a strong relationship your family members will be open to having you be part of their advisory boards and offering your input in assembling the remainder of their advisory boards.

Lifting by Contributing

When you cease to make a contribution, you begin to die.

—Eleanor Roosevelt

As with many high school students getting ready to graduate, my conversations with my high school friends revolved around discussing our plans after high school, including career choices. Our conversations centered around which careers would give us the greatest opportunity to be rich, sounded the most glamorous, and how those careers would eventually allow us to live the life of the rich and famous. Our conversations centered on what our careers can do for us. I don't recall many of our conversations being centered on what contributions we wanted to make in our careers.

Being a number of years removed from high school graduation, I have learned a few things about careers. I have learned, for example, that the market place is predominantly a lizard-brain, competitive, eat-or-be-eaten environment, and the structures and compensation systems are set up to perpetuate more of the same. I learned another important lesson early on in my career when I asked a wise mentor boss the definition of politics. He said politics is the art of self-preservation. I never forgot that definition. Much of the market place is a political environment that fosters more monkey-brain thinking of doing what is necessary to fit in even if it doesn't make sense—simply for the sake of self-preservation. These lizard-brain and monkey-brain systems would not exist if they didn't serve a useful purpose. However, they can go too far when such thinking dominates the work culture as it too often does.

It is not this way with every organization, team, or working person, however. Although success in the short run can be gained with a lizard-brain and monkey-brain mindset, work-life success in the long run will most likely be achieved with a divine-brain mindset of contribution. Such a divinative mindset will allow you to be successful in your work life, as well as simultaneously successful in your family life and personal life. You can't expect to have divine-brain thinking in the development of your character and your family while using predominantly lizard-brain and monkey-brain thinking at work. It will give you the sense that your life is misaligned.

One man cannot do right in one department of life whilst he is occupied in doing wrong in any other department. Life is one indivisible whole.

—Mahatma Gandhi

If you see in your workplace a predominantly lizard-brain and monkey-brain thinking environment, and it makes you feel uneasy, be grateful for that feeling. It is a signal that you want to have your divine brain be your dominant brain at work. Nearly every profession has components of contribution that everyone can focus on, but too often the significant contribution that can be made is blurred, and the point of focus is instead pointed in the direction of making money or playing internal politics. You may need to go in a different direction. A different direction might mean changing to a different industry, a different company, or it may mean you are in the right place, but you need to figure out how make your divine brain be more dominant at work through focusing on what contribution you would like to make in your chosen profession. Perhaps you have the positional power to make systemic changes and change the culture to one of contribution with less internal competition. Regardless of whichever change is appropriate for you, make the change—because piloting your life toward your life's mission depends on it.

The spirit of having the divine-brain mindset of contribution also applies in every role you may have outside of your work role, whether you are the soccer coach for your child's neighborhood team, a volunteer in your child's school, a leader in your church, or you are starting a part-time business. Focusing on contribution unleashes your creativity and passion for everything you do.

My object in living is to unite my avocation and my vocation as my two eyes make one in sight.

—Robert Frost

What do lifting your character, your capabilities, your family, and lifting by contributing in all your roles have to do with time management? Everything! This time management philosophy is not about making a long to-do list and seeing how many items you can check off your list in a day. This is about using your time with the intent to pilot your life to a culture of being more and not just doing more. This is about thinking like the most effective mothers and executives and discerning which activities, though they may be few in number, will have the greatest impact in your life. You have created your flight plan by creating your mission statement. By lifting and cultivating your character, your capabilities, your family, and by lifting other people in your other roles through the spirit of contribution you will be on your way to realizing your mission and being the person you want to be.

Attitude Indicator

From the simplest to the most sophisticated airplanes, there are certain gauges in the instrument panel that exist in all of them. The gauge in an instrumentation panel of a plane that lets the pilot know the orientation of the plane relative to the earth is called a gyro horizon or artificial horizon. Interestingly, it is also called an attitude indicator. The attitude indicator lets a pilot know whether the plane has the nose pointed down and the plane is moving downward towards the earth below, or whether the nose is pointed up and the plane is rising. Similarly, we can engage in activities we have outlined, that we know will lift and move us upward and forward toward our mission, or we can engage in other activities that weigh down our lives and direct our lives downward. Through this allegory you'll not only get a sense of where your attitude is currently heading but also what may be causing your attitude to be great or less than ideal.

The attitude indicator will also tell a pilot when the plane is rolling or tilted to the left or right as the plane turns. If the plane continues to turn in one direction, the plane will be traveling in a circle or oval shape. Some commercial flights will do this on purpose when they are waiting to get clearance from the air traffic controller to land. This is called a holding pattern. Have you ever felt that your life has been in a holding pattern?

This holding-pattern feeling we may have from time to time—in which we get the sense that our lives are not really moving forward—could happen in four ways. First, it could happen when you are not doing enough to lift yourself, while at the same time you are doing the best you can to lift your family and everyone else. I see this all too often with moms who, in the name of contribution to others, end up neglecting themselves and in time will be less able to lift their family or anyone else.

The second holding-pattern feeling can also happen when you are lifting yourself, your families, and others, but you may feel disconnected from the natural laws or principles or character that would give you the most direct route to the person you want to be. For example, I've heard mothers say in retrospect that although at times they may have lifted themselves physically through exercise and a healthy diet, lifted themselves emotionally through social activities, lifted themselves mentally through reading and study, they still felt weighed down. More than they cared to admit at the time, they approached life through the lizard-brain or monkey-brain mindset of competition and fitting in to the social norms at all costs. They later know down deep inside that their actions did not represent their best selves. Both of these scenarios of not doing enough to lift yourself or renew yourself toward your belief system, promises, vows, or covenants you have made, can create the feeling of being in a holding pattern in one direction.

Third, the holding-pattern feeling can also happen if you are not doing enough to lift your family. Like a plane that has lost an engine, when things are not going well on the home front, we lose power and speed, our progress is impeded, and we feel it. It is worth reminding all of us again that success at home is doing everything we can do to create the culture we want in the home. It doesn't guarantee that every member will respond to our wishes, because they each have the power to make their own choices. The point is making sure we do our part.

Fourth, it can also happen when we are not an active participant in the community at large. We all have an inward desire to contribute to the world we live in and to make a difference in our own unique ways. When we are not consciously and actively contributing and instead are sitting on the sidelines as a bystander, this can give you that holding-pattern feeling as well. We will provide you with a tool that you can use a tool to serve as an attitude indicator for your life. It will take the elements of all the allegories we have discussed and implement them.

Pulling It All Together

In your mind's eye, imagine looking at your current time-management tool, whether it is paper-based or electronic. In your imagination, remove from your current time-management tool everything that has dates and times. Furthermore, in your imagination remove the A-Z tabs where you record important names with their addresses, phone numbers, and e-mail addresses. After you have removed the pages with dates, times, as well as pages with important names and their useful information, what is left? If your answer is binder or nothing of significance, then what you have is a time-management tool. Our goal is much more than just a time-management tool, but a strategy to pilot and navigate your life to a culture of being more and not just doing more.

Structure

We recommend that when you open your paper-based planner, the first thing that you should see is your mission statement. Seeing it first every time you open your planner will be a constant reminder to you of your life's flight plan. If you have an electronic time management tool, have your mission statement easily accessible. On the following page is an example of what this page may look like. You will probably have additional pages as you revise and refine your mission statement. Your revisions will come as you gain additional insights about your unique divine life.

Mission Statement/Flight Plan Worksheet

Cultivate Character. What are at least three character traits you want to live by?

_____

_____

_____

Identify the personal goals and personal achievements you want just for you. If you were the last person left on earth, what personal goals would you set just for your personal satisfaction?

_____

_____

_____

Create Family Culture. From your gut, what do you want your family culture to be like?

_____

_____

_____

Contribute to Community. With your unique talents, gifts, and interests, what are the contributions that you would like to make at work, your community, your church, and in other roles you may have?

_____

_____

_____

The next items you should see are tabs for each of the areas of focus of your life. Have a tab for character, capabilities, family, and contribution. Within each tab is contained the ideas you have read in this book. Additionally, within each tab is where you will write down ideas of things you may choose to do in the future. For example, have you ever been driving down the road or going for a walk, and out of nowhere comes a flash of a brilliant idea? Maybe a great idea comes to mind that you had not yet considered. Perhaps you have questions you have been pondering for quite some time, and then the answer finally comes to you. Where do you typically put those ideas? Have you ever been in a work conference, and you come up with an insight that can positively affect your family? Where do you put those ideas? Instead of just organizing your time-management tool strictly by time, have your time-management tool also organized according to each of the areas of focus of your life. Have a place where you collect your insights, flashes of brilliant ideas, and inspired goals. Along with these insights you may collect, write down specific areas of your life that you feel need special focus, such as patience, kindness, or being a better listener. To get you started on what your collection of brilliant activities might look like, consider the following questions and write down a few ideas. Don't worry about how you might accomplish them at this point. Just jot down your ideas. This is your wish list.

For your work life (or for any role that you might have in your life in the community at large, such as a church role, coaching role, volunteer role, etcetera), what do you want to have happen that is not now happening?

_____

_____

_____

What do you want to have happen that is not now happening in your family life?

_____

_____

_____

_____

In a global economy where change is happening in an ever-accelerating speed, assume that your current skills will be obsolete in a couple of years. What new skill sets would you like to develop? What new knowledge would you need to and want to acquire?

_____

_____

_____

_____

What do you want to have happen that is not now happening in your personal life? What character traits would you like to develop?

_____

_____

_____

_____

The following page is a sample of what a page in your character tab may look like.

AREA OF FOCUS: CHARACTER

How can I cultivate and strengthen my character?

- What do I really want? Have the deep desire to be my best self.
- Commit to be divinative and begin and end my day with prayer or meditation as well as read scriptures or inspirational literature.
- Remember the zigzag path to growth. Growing pains are just part of the process.
- Pre-forgive myself along the way.
- Assemble my advisory board.
- Assess my successes and setbacks through the Achievement Cycle, and make the appropriate adjustments.
- Identify and then reduce or eliminate lizard-brain and monkey-brain activities.
- Learn from without, then grow from within.

What else do I want to have happen that is not now happening in strengthening my character? What should I continue doing, stop doing, and start doing to make it so?

_____

_____

_____

_____

_____

Here is a sample of what a page in your family tab may look like.

AREA OF FOCUS: FAMILY

How can I lift members of my family?

- Help my family to be divinative by my example, and encourage them to begin and end their days using their divine brains.
- Read scriptures or inspirational literature and monitor for any early-troubling warning signs.
- Pre-forgive.
- Listen with the intent to hear, and appreciate their splendor, honor, and glory.
- Expand their vision with patience.
- Speak words and display acts of kindness.
- Help my children assemble their advisory boards.

What else do I want to have happen that is not now happening in my family life? What should I continue doing, stop doing, and start doing to make it so?

_____

_____

_____

_____

_____

After your mission statement and individual tabs for each of the areas of focus of your life, the next vitally important part of your time-management tool is your weekly plan. Nearly every time-management tool in the market is designed for a one-year time frame, whether it begins in the calendar year or you purchase them in the beginning of a quarter. Nearly every time-management tool in the market has a monthly calendar to jot down your upcoming events months in advance. Nearly every time-management tool in the market has a daily calendar to put down your to-do list for each day, and you can organize your tasks and appointments in the appropriate time. However, many time management tools aren't organized by the week.

For most people a week means a seven-day period, but historically a week has ranged anywhere between a three-day to a ten-day week in different parts of the world. The Aztecs and Maya even had a thirteen-day week. The length of the week is not as important as much as what the week represents. The week represents the shortest cycle of living. For our purposes we'll define the week as a seven-day period. In this seven-day cycle of living, your activities during the weekend tend to be different from your activities in the weekday. Even within your weekdays your activities on Mondays are different from your activities on Thursdays and so on. The totality of this seven-day week represents the shortest cycle of living. Think of piloting and navigating your life in increments of a week. We'll cover the weekly planning process and a tool you can use that we refer to as a weekly attitude indicator.

Weekly Planning Process

- Review your flight plan or mission.
- Review how much you moved towards your mission during the past week and celebrate and/or pre-forgive yourself.
- Review possible activities from your areas of focus tabs. Come up with your goals that you will implement in the coming week to lift each area of focus within your life and write them down in your weekly attitude indicator.
- Transfer your goals to your calendar.
- Report and give an accounting to your accountability adviser.

Sometime between Friday afternoon and Sunday evening block out fifteen to twenty minutes to plan your coming week. In your planning time, first think in terms of your mission or your life's flight plan. Reconnect. Be inspired and renewed by your mission and what you want to do and be in your life. Remember from the loom analogy that you are trying to improve both your warp of character and your weft of goals and activities.

After reviewing your mission, think about the week before. Did you move closer to your mission? As you review the areas of focus in your life (your character, your capabilities, your family, and your roles in the community at large) did you do your part to lift each of these areas of focus, or were you weighed down in some? Celebrate those areas you were able to lift! There is not enough celebration going on for significant weekly accomplishments that bring you closer to your mission. Raise both arms in air and congratulate yourself! In those areas where you were weighed down, remember the principle of pre-forgiveness. You have a divine nature and divine potential, and you have the upcoming week to make improvements.

The next step is to review ideas from this book that you would capture in the areas of focus tabbed sections in your time-management tool. There may be additional ideas you have written down. The concept is to continually add to the list, other ideas and goals that will help you lift yourself and others. For the coming week you may consider goals from the list you have written on your areas of focus tabs or by simply reviewing your list, you will probably come up with other thoughts and ideas.

The next step is to choose your goals for the week. Thinking specifically of this week, ask yourself what should you continue doing, start doing, and stop doing that will lift each of the areas of focus in your life. On the next page, you will see what your weekly attitude indicator will look like.

After you fill out your weekly attitude indicator, think for a moment about what your week would be like if you were able to accomplish everything on your weekly attitude indicator. If the goals you have written down are goals that you feel will truly lift your character, capabilities, your family, and help you improve the contributions you are making in other roles of your life, it will give you a sense of moving towards your mission. In those cases when you only accomplish part of the goals you have written down on your weekly attitude indicator, you should still feel pretty good because you are making deliberate strides towards your mission. If you find that in certain weeks you are not able to finish everything you have set out to do in your weekly attitude indicator, pre-forgive yourself and try it again the following week.

WEEKLY ATTITUDE INDICATOR

Climbing left bank   Straight climb   Climbing right bank

AREAS OF FOCUS AND GOALS FOR THIS WEEK

Week of: _____ Accountability Adviser: _____

Strengthen Character

_____

_____

Increase Capabilities

_____

_____

Lift My Family

_____

_____

Improve Contribution

_____

_____

Other Areas of Focus

_____

_____

In the early 1900s an Italian economist, Vilfredo Pareto, came up with a mathematical formula to describe the unequal distribution of wealth in his country. He observed that 80 percent of the wealth was held by 20 percent of the population. In the 1930s and 1940s a management consultant, Joseph Juran, recognized a principle he called "the vital few and the trivial many." He asserted that 20 percent of something is responsible for 80 percent of the results. This 80/20 rule has applications in many areas. For example, you may find 20 percent of your sales staff produces 80 percent of your sales. You may also find that 20 percent of your work consumes 80 percent of your time and resources. I would suggest that in the field of time management, similar conclusions can be made. There are the "vital few" activities that can have a tremendous impact on how you use your time and thus lead you to be the person you want to be. The goals you select in your weekly attitude indicator are intended to be the "vital few" goals or perhaps the 20 percent of your activities that will facilitate 80 percent of the results. As a mother or any other executive, focus on the power of the vital few and not the length of to-do lists. Separate the impactful few from the immediate many.

The last step of your weekly planning process is to let your account-ability adviser know how your last week went and what your goals are for the coming week. This need not be a long process. Remember that the prob-ability of completing your goals go up to 95 percent when you have a specific appointment with your accountability adviser and give an accounting of your progress. Choose an accountability adviser whom you trust and is willing to help you reach your goals and be the person you want to be.

Daily Planning

After you have filled out your weekly attitude indicator, transfer your goals to your calendar. Some of your goals can be easily transferred, while others may be areas of focus that you look for opportunities to implement. For example, if one of your goals is to be more patient, this is not a goal you will narrow down to a day and time, but it's something you will work on throughout the week. Schedule the goals in your weekly attitude indicator first, and then plan the remainder of the week.

I have found that daily planning will vary with each person's style, schedule load, detail orientation, personality, and complexity in the family, nature of work, and number of roles outside of home and work. The essence of daily planning is making sure you have written down all of your appointments, so you don't forget. You will also jot down your to-do list, which is not time-specific as your appointments are. After you have created your to-do list, put an "M" next to those items on your to-do list that you must do, an "S" next to those you should do and a "C" next to those you could do. Prioritize and number all of the items you must do, so you'll have M1, M2, M3, and so forth. Do the same thing with the should-do list and your could-do list. Do the must-do items first, followed by the should-do list, and lastly the could-do list if you have time. Check each item off as you do it, because it feels good.

If you have a different process for daily planning that you like, do that. You will more than likely gravitate towards a system that feels comfortable to you on daily planning. There is more than one right way to do daily planning. You will always be struggling with how much is too much to try to tackle in one day, and how much is not enough. Think back to the all-you-can-eat buffet analogy. Metaphorically speaking, get enough done so that you get your money's worth, but not so much that you get that bloated, "I shouldn't have done that" feeling. Regardless of whether or not you have the proper balance in your daily planning, what is infinitely more important is meeting the goals you put in your weekly attitude indicator. Think like a highly-effective and happy executive and/or mom. Congratulate yourself for getting the big stuff done—the vital and impactful few items that lead you to your mission—and don't sweat the never-ending smaller stuff.

Consider what you accomplish each time you live according to your goals in your weekly attitude indicator. You will have piloted your life to a culture of being more and not just doing more. That was the goal. You will come out of that holding-pattern feeling. You will weave your warp of character and weft of activities and goals, and you will help your family members do the same. You will make improved contributions in your other roles.

You are divine. A mother's (and father's) work is priceless. The role of a parent is the most important role any person can have. The impact of parenting is immediate and will last for generations. I express my deepest appreciation for moms all over the world. You are wonderful. You are a living inspiration.

This has been quite a journey (or flight) that we have taken together. This has been more than just about time, time management, or time-management tools. It is really about knowing how to use time to deliberately weave life.

> Where is the Life we have lost in living? Where is the wisdom we have lost in knowledge? Where is the knowledge we have lost in information?
>
> —T.S. Elliot